*The strength of a warrior is not solely in the armor she wears.*
*Her strength often comes from the burdens she bears!*

Khris

# Dedication

For Kierstin and Kerrigan for being my reasons why, the possibilities of, and the moments when God designed my destiny.

# Your Destiny Begins with Identity

## 30 THINGS GOD WANTS EVERY GIRL TO KNOW NOW

## Khris Ferland

TRILOGY CHRISTIAN PUBLISHERS

*Tustin, CA*

Trilogy Christian Publishers
A Wholly Owned Subsidary of Trinity Broadcasting Network
2442 Michelle Drive
Tustin, CA 92780

*Your Desitiny Begins with Identity: 30 Things God Wants Every Girl to Know Now*

For information, address Trilogy Christian Publishing

Rights Department, 2442 Michelle Drive, Tustin, Ca 92780.

Trilogy Christian Publishing/ TBN and colophon are trademarks of Trinity Broadcasting Network.

For information about special discounts for bulk purchases, please contact Trilogy Christian Publishing.

Trilogy Disclaimer: The views and content expressed in this book are those of the author and may not necessarily reflect the views and doctrine of Trilogy Christian Publishing or the Trinity Broadcasting Network.

10 9 8 7 6 5 4 3 2 1

Library of Congress Cataloging-in-Publication Data is available.

ISBN 979-8-89041-849-4

ISBN 979-8-89041-850-0 (ebook)

# Acknowledgments

The husband who held me up on the tireless days and the darkest of nights. Your encouragement, support, and never-ending love are why our family stands firmly, empowered, and beautifully. Thank you for the season you carried the three of us on your back, lifting your eyes to the heavens for the strength and talking to God the whole time.

Thirty mothers of daughters, who, when asked to be a part of this project, responded with a resounding yes and whose voices echo through the pages of this book applauding their daughters.

A sister of two sons who allowed me to mother one of them for a season, teaching me what it's like to love a boy.

My mom, whose life was the epitome of how to love Jesus.

My dad, whose life's work was all about Jesus.

The friend who didn't think it was crazy when I sat in my closet in my home, and she sat in her closet in her home across town, as we prayed together over the phone many times for my daughters and her sons. Thank you for "understanding me."

The friend whose daughter left earth way too soon but now rests in the arms of Jesus. You are brave and courageous and lovely. I'm happy to hold you up.

# Contents

# Foreword

When Khris first asked if I would write the foreword for her new book, she was reluctant to do so because I am a mother to boys. She humorously yet sincerely stated she had been in prayer about whom to ask and was awakened by the Holy Spirit during the middle of the night that I was that person. To know Khris is to know that after hearing how profoundly God answered her prayer, your best response is to accept. She is a woman of great faith and a passionate prayer. Throughout my years of knowing her, she has been a pillar of strength during moments when I needed encouragement, listening intently to my heart and praying for me. Often, she would provide scriptures, God's word, about my situation. There has never been a time when I haven't experienced the power of God working through her to yield favorable outcomes for me and my family. These qualities of faith and prayer are the inspiration for this book.

As someone who has experienced various forms of brokenness, I know the value and significance of gaining God's perspective. Reflecting on the potential impact of this book on my own life as an emergent teenager and during my college years brought tears to my eyes. In a time where women have been empowered to achieve the unimaginable, there is also a prevalent degradation of women by others and even by themselves. Therefore, the truth in Khris's words is crucial. The Spirit and love that God has for you are infused throughout the pages, and undoubtedly you will feel them!

I first met Khris over fifteen years ago when her oldest daughter and my oldest son attended the same private Christian school in a Dallas suburb. As our friendship evolved, I got to know her and her compassionate heart for girls and women at a greater level. This book is not about seeking popularity. It is Khris's calling to touch the hearts of young girls to empower them to confidently embrace the women God has fashioned them to be. Whether you have a biological daughter or a spiritual daughter or you're a father raising a daughter, it's vital to recognize that at some point she may grapple with her identity. The good news is that the Word of God addresses every concern about her. Khris effectively and powerfully guides girls to align with God to fulfill their destiny, which no one else has the power to orchestrate.

You may ask, "Why does God want me to know this now?" The reason is that *you* were created for a unique purpose. The Bible says before you were born, He had determined in advance why *you* are here. This book will confirm that you are valued! It will also strengthen you because everything is based upon the Bible, which is the blueprint for our life.

And as you read these truths that God wants you to know, my prayer is that your life will be forever transformed through the renewal of your mind.

I would be remiss if I did not honor my mother, Bettie Scott, who is a true pioneer and warrior woman. I am certain that I wouldn't have a minute chance of being the person that I am today if she had not activated the call on her life and walked out her God-given identity.

In Him,
Tia Lane Texada

# Preface

Maybe you haven't heard it before, but I've heard it countless times, especially when the person saying it has experienced something so unsuspecting and so sweetly contradictory to the facts of a matter. It's usually when someone has been waiting on God and has finally resigned to giving up, and then a blessing comes seemingly out of nowhere, or, in my case, a miracle happens. And yes, there's a difference between a blessing and a miracle. A miracle operates outside of rules and is God intervening supernaturally. Whereas a blessing comes naturally. Along a natural pathway.

"God's timing is perfect!" How many times have you heard that or said it yourself because God showed up at a moment's notice? This book is about God's timing being perfect. Absolutely perfect!

The first time "God's perfect timing" came for me was when I was nineteen years old and my parents were told I would never have children because of a medical condition. This condition rendered me infertile. Well, 99 percent infertile, my mom was told. So after we were married, my husband and I never tried to become pregnant. We never prayed to become pregnant. Why would we? We accepted the "facts of the matter" and began to build a life with each other and God at the center. I mean, 99 percent is like saying 100 percent. Then unsuspectingly, surprisingly, and unexpectedly, I became pregnant with my first daughter. A miracle! God's supernatural intervention penetrated the circumstances of my life, defying logic and science. Twice! Now two girls later. I have a friend, Darcy, who describes moments like these when God intervenes and changes the course of things in a moment's notice. In the twinkling of an eye.

Throughout the years of mothering my daughters, I began to research the dynamic of girls, what it means to be a girl, the personality of girls, what concerns girls, the progression to womanhood, and a myriad of other things. In my desperation to be a good mother to daughters I really wasn't supposed to bear according to science, I took my time, at every stage of their lives, to figure out how the mothering of girls is done. I implemented some of what the books and experts said and what I innately felt and packaged it together wrapping it in what God said.

The most fundamental, foundational, and profound thing I learned was that girls are born with an innermost, nuclear beauty that shows through their hearts and becomes the thread that weaves through their spirits. Their value is noted not in what they look like but in how they approach and navigate the circumstances in their sphere as they develop and their sphere expands. But how do girls learn to navigate life? Through a mother's and father's guidance and whose foundation is based on what God says.

I also found, through research, that language is the most fundamental foundation of civilization.[1] It designs society, and the female is more adept at learning language and has greater word power than their male peers. Did you know this? What does this mean for the power of the female that the thing that structures, builds, and sustains the world, girls possess a greater measure of it? It means girls are charged with taking that authority and power, combining it with their passions, and leading in their areas of expertise to build the world and the kingdom of God.

This is why there is a designed, unrelenting, ever-mutating attack on the world's girls by society, and it's certainly nothing to be afraid of but definitely something to be acknowledged and made aware of. This attack is calculated and guided by the spiritual realm because the greatest enemy knows that girls are special and hold special assignments ordained by Father God. The enemy also knows that when God ordains something, it will inevitably be cloaked in success. Girls hold and possess the ability to produce the next generation of girls who will be the changemakers in society too. No one else can do this except girls.

Given this, I wanted to make sure my daughters and the world's daughters knew the power they have, so this book is for them and their daughters and for generations of daughters to come. That overt and blatant attack on the world's girls is nothing to cower to. Girl, gather up all that you are in this moment of your life and come with me as God reveals your identity for the road to your destiny!

# Introduction

My seventeen-year-old daughter and I were talking about her imminent entry into the world of college life. It was not to happen for a year, but I wanted to be sure as a mom I was covering all the bases in talking to her about everything I hadn't gotten around to talking to her about and driving home those things I had talked to her about. We were having a great time laughing a lot. Though at some points Kierstin was aghast at a few topics I was brave enough to pursue. Then after several minutes of me braving the water waste deep, she grew serious, the look on her beautiful face full of sadness and wonder. She said to me, "Mom, how will I know what to do when you're not there? What if something happened to you and I can't talk to you? Who will help me?"

Then I grew serious, and my heart was full of love for her at the thought of my beautiful girls growing into young women without me. I shuddered in protest, declaring that Almighty God would cover me and grant me the longevity of life so that I could see their triumphs, lift them when they fall, applaud them when they achieve, and embrace them when they need. My sweet girl must have noticed the pained look on my own face because then she said, "Mom, can you write it all down so that I will always know what to do?" I thought to myself, *Well, there's an idea!* Then I said, "You bet I will! I will write it all down!" I began to write *Letters to My Christian Daughters* but quickly realized that I was actually writing these letters to all girls and these letters would teach them about identity and destiny.

So *Your Destiny Begins with Identity: 30 Things God Wants Every Girl to Know Now* is born of that moment when my baby girl felt a sense of urgency about wanting to know how she should navigate different situations in her life, a life on a journey to young womanhood. Now, don't get me wrong. I empower my girls to make their own choices in life, but this book is a conversation I would have with them on a myriad of different topics, a conversation between mother and daughter. It's a roadmap to navigate the prepubescent through emerging adulthood to guide girls as they transition into young womanhood based on the Word of our Father. This book will bridge the gap between the point girls are questioning who they are and their roles in life and evolving into young women changemakers ready to make a difference in the world.

My husband and I often take turns leading our girls in kitchen table Bible study. We encourage them to read the Word of God daily. And not on an iPad or cell phone but leather-bound Bibles they can hold in their hands, highlight important scriptures, and flip the pages. My own mother encouraged me in the same way. I still use the Bible my parents bought me the day I left for college! It's tattered and worn, but I can't imagine using anything else to study the Word of God.

*Your Destiny Begins with Identity: 30 Things God Wants Every Girl to Know Now* is my heart leaping at the warmth I feel hearing my own voice in my head speaking the truth to my daughters. It's seeing their eyes wide with anticipation as they sit with me listening to hear what God will say, hanging on my every word. That's why it's important for me to ensure every word leaving my mouth aligns with God's Word.

As you read this book, you will laugh at the lions outside our home, cry with me over pony rides, yearn for solitude, and imagine your life with Almighty God.

Mothers, perhaps there are letters you wish your mother had written to you. What did you need her to say? What do you wish she had said, explained, introduced, or opened up a discussion about? Mothers, maybe you are thinking about this book for your daughter. Use it as a tool to begin many discussions I know in the end will forge a bond so great between you and your daughter and your daughter and God that He will be exalted in ways you can't imagine. Watch her grow into the young woman of God He created her to be as a result of you and her bonding over these letters.

Not a day goes by I am not in awe of who my daughters are becoming. The depth of their characters leaves me transfixed on how they are becoming who they are. Sure, my husband and I laid a great foundation for them, but there came a moment in time when they began to seek Jesus for themselves. They wanted their own relationship with Him. Their reliance on His promises shone through in the risks they took, the courage they mustered in challenging times, and the brave hearts they grew in the face of adversity. I no longer recognized them as my babies but as young women of God who were unashamed to claim Him and unrelenting in pursuit of Him! My heart danced at the realization of that!

Mothers, if you are giving this book to your daughter(s), please do this exercise.

I have designated an area on the last page of this book for you to write a letter to your daughter. Write about anything you like, but begin by praying and asking God to infuse the words you write with His voice and Spirit. Take a few days to pray while asking the Father what you should say. Speak directly to her and write from your heart.

If you don't have a daughter and you know a young girl whose mother is no longer on this earth, please write a letter to her before you give her this book. This exercise is designed to help you discover the power of the words that are in your heart for your daughters and the world's daughters. When you give this book to your daughter, be sure to show her the letter you wrote to her.

If you are a daughter and have stumbled upon this book, you will write a letter to your mother, writing about what you hope to gain through this book as well as thanking her for her presence in your life.

This is your journey to self-discovery! This book was designed especially with you in mind as you are seeking your place in this world and deciding to live every moment of your time on earth to the glory of the Father. You will begin to feel the urging of God to listen to each word and measure them against what your life looks like and what it can evolve into in the presence of God. You will learn the power of words, discarding the ones that devalue you and donning the ones that celebrate you!

After each chapter is an interactive section I have titled "Wearing Emeralds." I chose this title because emeralds are green, and green symbolizes growth and new beginnings. My prayer for you, daughter, is that you will take this new beginning and grow in your relationship with the Father, with yourself, and with the world as you empower yourself to leave your footprint here on earth.

Use the "Wearing Emeralds" section to answer the questions and directives after reading the preceding chapter. Approach this exercise with everything you have learned in the chapter, building commitments to utilize the information to grow your relationship with God and with yourself. I challenge you to wear your emeralds every day.

Now, mothers, turn to the last page of this book and write a letter to your daughter. Daughters, write a letter to your mother. And then begin this journey that will embolden you and those in your circle to embrace the power of these words!

Khris

Jennifer Hannah
For Sydney

*"You are enough. Like Esther, you have been uniquely created to be seen and heard for such a time as this. God will supply your needs and meet you where you are. Just ask Him."*

## CHAPTER 1

# Your Identity

Who Do You Think You Are?

*Lionhearted*

Dear Daughter, identity includes so many different facets of a person, ranging from physical traits to personality traits, where we come from, and who our family is. As we grow, some of those traits are constantly evolving, which can cause us to identify ourselves differently over time. But when the foundation of who we are is rooted in who God says we are, our identity looks much like what He looks like. Our identity is born from our relationship with Him. So it shapes what we believe, what we stand for, and what we are gifted to do. Everyone, at some point in life, will ask themselves, "Who am I?" When this happens, be ready for the sequence of events that will begin your journey of self-discovery and exploring self-identity. This can take form in a myriad of different ways, but a few things could lead you to that moment.

1. You will begin to feel unsettled from within, like you were meant for more than how you are currently living, not passionate about what you are doing. Like something is missing.
2. An event could happen that will cause you to question what it means for your life.
3. An opportunity will seemingly come out of nowhere, one that gets you excited about navigating the possibility of a new opportunity.

This all means that it is time to self-reflect and start your journey to identity. *Your journey to destiny begins with identity.*

It was a typical morning after carpool, and I was to meet a couple of friends for breakfast at a spot we frequented after dropping our kids off at school. I was feeling a little uneasy, unenthused, and lethargic in my mind. I was tired of the routine, living this day over and over knowing I was meant for more. But what? What was more? That question had been haunting me for a couple of years, expecting me to know the answer, and each year I didn't. Here it was another school year, and I still didn't know. I didn't know when I was going to know, and because of that, I slid into the routine of a typical morning after carpool.

When I arrived at the restaurant, I immediately saw my two friends whose backs were to me as I walked toward the table we usually sat at. It was our favorite because it gave us a view of the lake. We were always fortunate to sit there because we weren't the only moms who had dropped their kids off at school, headed for this restaurant, and spent the morning talking. I often wondered if some of the other moms felt like I felt. I didn't know. Neither of my friends noticed when I approached, and I heard one of them ask the other, "Does Khris seem different to you?"

"Yes!" the other exclaimed. "She's very quiet and not wanting to hang out much. She's turned down several lunch invitations. I'm not asking her anymore. Like who does she think she is!" There were those words that had traipsed through my mind like a butterfly dancing above a field of clover. I know my friends weren't being malicious, but their words caused an overflow of tears in my eyes and just plain old hurt in my heart. It wasn't their fault I had come to a place in my life where I knew I needed more and the same old day-in and day-out was no longer enough for me. I turned and left for the comfort of my car to cry the ugly cry of sorts, so I did. That had hurt, but I think the tears that wouldn't stop were more for the fact that I didn't know who I was. My friend asked in a harmless, matter-of-fact way. But I asked God out of desperation and a harrowing ache in my heart. I immediately drove home to find out who I was. I was determined that by the time I was to pick the girls up from school, I would undoubtedly know who I was and what I was placed on planet Earth to do. But I didn't find out that day. It doesn't work that way. No one tells us that it's a journey and that it would take more time and introspection.

Identity is the driving force of what a person's contribution to the world will be, so it's important to get there. I had wasted enough time. God has a way of allowing things that hurt us to get our attention about things he has been telling us all along. For me, it was that I was meant for more. That day I was set on a journey to find out what more looked like for me.

It wasn't a coincidence that a few days later I heard my daughters going at it.

"Who do you think you are, just taking my jeans and wearing them without asking?" This time the two of them were arguing bitterly.

"I find my things you never ask my permission to wear in your laundry basket all the time, and I don't get angry!" That was Kerrigan, my then twelve-year-old, on the responding end this time. She and her sixteen-year-old sister Kierstin often use the phrase, "Who do you think you are?" in heated moments when one has offended the other in some way.

The girls aren't interested in knowing who the other thinks she is. What's happening here are hints of sarcasm, and they use the phrase to accuse the other person of thinking more highly of herself, more highly than others may view her. This statement requires an unraveling, a disengaging. The Bible states in Romans 12:3, "For through the grace given to me, I say to everyone among you, not to think more highly of himself than he ought to think; but to think to have sound judgment, as God has allotted to each a measure of faith."

Here, the apostle Paul is indeed instructing us not to brag about ourselves and the God-given gifts we have. But we only read the first part of that verse in heated moments, hurling it insultingly at others. But do you understand what the second part of that verse means? It means to never disparage yourself as if God has given you nothing! It means to walk in the gifts and talents God has given you. It means allowing those gifts and talents to live out loud in you. When you are filled with the presence of God, and that is coupled with using the gifts and talents He has given you, you absolutely should think more highly of yourself because you are holding in your possession one of the most sacred of things God has given you—what you are to use on earth to build the kingdom in heaven. God, in His infinite glory, thinks more highly of you, and as young women of God, you are made in His image.

Thinking more highly of yourself in the name of the Father says you are not willing to risk your life, future, or relationship with God for anything. What it says about you is that you think you are too valuable to waste your time and talents on anything outside of the divine purpose for your life. So the next time someone asks you, "Who do you think you are?" what will you say?

Should we, as girls, emphasize who others say we are? There is only one truth to how you are defined: the Truth Himself. Any other definition of who you are that detracts from what God says is a lie.

Have you ever asked yourself the question "Who am I?" and come up with an answer other than your name? Or has any-one ever asked you, "Who do you think you are?"? Who are you? Who do you want to be? Are you on the path to being who you want to be or who God wants you to be? Are the two the same?

When you ask yourself these questions, the process can set you on that journey I mentioned earlier. The one that causes you to really delve into your heart, mind, and spirit and can introduce you to yourself. The self you don't yet realize is there: your brave self, your formidable self, your fearless self, your gifted self, your Almighty self! And the capital letter A on the word almighty in the previous sentence is not a mistake. It symbolizes Jesus as the Almighty. Because Almighty lives in you, making you Almighty as well.

As you navigate life, it's important to ask yourself these questions because, in doing so, the answers will ignite your self-introspection. Oftentimes, as we are introspective, we learn things about ourselves that help us grow. You are constantly evolving and to completely know who you are at this age is impossible! Beginning to explore what interests you, your likes and dislikes, and your position in your relationships is the beginning of you getting to know yourself. And although it's impossible to completely know who you are at this age, what you can decide is to know who God says you are right now and what that means for your future.

> "But as many as received Him, to them He gave the right to become children of God, even to those who believe in His name."
>
> John 1:12

Learning now that you are a child of God is the single most important thing you could learn about yourself. It truly is because, as a child of God, His Word tells you everything you will need to know about life—your life. It will help you grow in shaping your character, which is why it's imperative to read the Bible on a regular basis. Otherwise, how will you know which direction to take in different circumstances of your life? It really is a roadmap for life.

Don't fall into the trap of believing the Bible was written so long ago that it's not relevant for your life today. Yes, it was written many years ago, but its relevance transcends time. God foreknew the same issues and problems our biblical ancestors faced would be the same issues we would face today. The Bible reminds us that God is the same yesterday, today, and forevermore. When He inspired the prophets to write the Bible, it was indeed as well for such a time as now.

I remember one Saturday, on the sideline of one of my daughter's soccer games, I was in a discussion with another mom about a topic that was making headlines in the news almost daily. It was an election year, and each presidential candidate was, of course, on opposite sides of this issue. The mom I was talking to asked who I was going to vote for, which I felt was a bit personal. I circumvented the question by trying to change the subject, but she was unrelenting. She obviously joined the millions of people across the country wanting to voice their opinion about the topic. Abortion. Everyone was talking about it wherever I went—the grocery store, the bank, the dry cleaners, restaurants. For several minutes I allowed her to explain her position on abortion, never interrupting, just listening. When it was my turn to offer my position, I explained what my thoughts were, which aligned with the Word of God. I further explained what the Bible said about abortion and how I could understand the anxiety and burden a woman must feel about having to decide about an unwanted pregnancy but further declared that I was resolute in my position, as it echoes the Bible. She then said to me very incredulously and chuckling condescendingly, "Come on, Khris! Really? Do you really believe everything the Bible says?" My heart sank for her, and my mouth was agape. I was flabbergasted to learn this mother did not believe the truth of the Bible. Nor did she believe it was relevant for today. She went on to explain to me that the Bible was written for people who lived in "Bible times"—that the world has evolved so much so that we as humans must change with it and can't possibly live with a book like the Bible as our standard! My heart broke for her as I wondered what her life must have been like choosing only to believe the Bible on some things and not others. She must be massively confused! Like, how does she choose from the Bible what to believe and what not to believe? Does she sit down at her kitchen table and pick straws from the broom to decide, with the longest straw winning? Or maybe the shortest straw winning? Does she ask someone else what they think and then goes with whatever their answer maybe? Or does she decide based on how far-fetched she believes or not the story in the Bible sounds? Is she relying on her own worldview instead of the Christian worldview? How does she decide what in the Bible to believe and what not to believe?

You beautiful daughters, everything in the Bible is true and as real as the sun shining each day! In fact, the sun that shines today is the same sun that shone in 'Bible times'! When God created the sun, He didn't create it only for the time in which He created it. The Bible is the inspired word of God, and He is the Father of truth, not lies. Stand firm in believing what God says about everything. Stand firm in believing in who God says you are! Don't allow the world, friends, teachers, and coaches to define who you are when the Most High Sovereign God of the universe already has! You are His, and He is sending you out into the world to take part in making the world a better place for us all. The world needs the greatness you possess.

When you are being introspective, digging deeply into the Word of God, and learning who you are, know that God says you are His. "But as many as received Him, to them He gave the right to become children of God, to those who believe in His name" (John 1:12). There are a myriad of scriptures in the Bible defining who you are, and each one points to God being your Father.

Psalm 139:14 says you are fearfully and wonderfully made; Ephesians 2:10 says you are His workmanship created in Jesus; Genesis 1:27 says you are made in His image; 1 Corinthians 3:16 says you are God's temple and His Spirit dwells in you. I can go on and on about what the Bible says about who you are, so before you believe how others define you, go quickly to the Word of the Father and begin there. Align your thinking with God's thinking. What you will find once you begin to do this on a regular basis is empowerment! Yes! You will be so strong and unmovable that you will feel empowered. That's what the Word of God does. It empowers us and gives us the authority we need to live unshaken lives so that we positively affect the lives of others.

Let's talk for a moment about what identity is not. Identity is not the result of the person you are after you've made mistakes. In other words, you are not your mistakes. There's something about mistakes that are unique to every living soul on earth. We all have a story or two to tell about the mistakes we've made. If you are alive, you have made mistakes, and if you continue to live, you will continue to make them. There are endless numbers of mistakes people make. The unique thing about the mistakes we make is that as we grow in our relationship with the Father, the types of mistakes are less powerful over our lives and we adopt a standard of behavior that is based on His Word, affecting the choices we make.

You are not your failures. But why do we feel so deeply and hurt so badly after we've made a mistake or failed at something if we're not our mistakes or failures? Because in the moment of the hurt and after mistakes we've made, we sometimes don't have the capacity to self-encourage. Learning to self-encourage after mistakes and what we consider failures is key to defining who you are. Practice encouraging yourself after you've made a mistake or you think you have failed at something. When you do, you remove the enemy's power over you.

So, when someone asks you, "Who do you think you are?" you can respond resoundingly that you are the daughter of the King of kings, the Lord of lords, Ruler of heaven and earth, the All-Powerful, Majestic God of the universe. And when you say it, say it with the authority that is yours!

## Wearing Emeralds

In your own words, explain who you are without using your name. Describe those things you think define who you are.

_____

_____

_____

_____

_____

_____

_____

_____

_____

_____

_____

_____

_____

_____

_____

_____

_____

_____

_____

_____

_____

## Word Power

Lionhearted: *Very brave, determined.*

Describe a time you were faced with a challenge and you needed to be brave and determined for an outcome that would make you feel satisfied with and proud of yourself.

_____

_____

_____

_____

_____

_____

_____

_____

_____

_____

_____

_____

_____

_____

_____

_____

_____

Susan Donohue
For Katie, Christine, and Bridget

*"Listen to your body. It is wiser than your years."*

# CHAPTER 2

# Your Body

*Strong*

Dear Daughter, our skin comprises our body, being its largest organ and its most visible. When others look at us, it's our bodies they use first to make assumptions about who they think we are. Our self-image, how we take care of our bodies, and how we adorn them are a large part of our identity, which I previously wrote about. What do you think about your body, and how did those thoughts originate?

The human body, in all of its intricacy, holds so much influence over what we think of ourselves. We sometimes think the thoughts we have about ourselves are original ones. Sometimes they're not. They can originate from outside of ourselves too. It begins very early on and can last a lifetime; the agenda of the culture is to influence our thoughts about our bodies so that whatever tools it uses to do so, we become reliant on and customers of in perpetuity.

But what's wrong with using a product or service that works for you? One making a claim that you've found value and validity in. Nothing. The problem is that we allow the product being sold to us to determine how we should feel about our image, leaving ourselves open to negative thoughts about our bodies. Thoughts about ourselves are powerful and are the difference between a successful or failed journey to self-discovery. It is your responsibility to decide that your body belongs to you and begin to affirm your body, flaws and all. Your body is a very important part of who you are and what makes you authentically you. It functions to serve who you are so that you can more effectively make your impact in the world. When you look at yourself in the mirror, know the curves of your body, the color of your skin, your eye color and hair color, and the size of your hands and feet were all made by God specifically to make you who you are. He took the time to carve you, make you, and mold you into what you looked like at birth to grow into what you look like today.

Early on, as a teenager, I learned a valuable lesson in taking care of my body. I ran track in middle and high school. I wasn't as serious about it as my teammates. It was simply an opportunity for me to be social because all my friends were doing it, and they were doing it for the same reason as I was: to have fun being social. Eventually, I became pretty good at a sport I didn't fully engage in mentally but was, truth be told, just having fun. It worked for me. Until one day our coach, who trained runners for the 200 meters, called me to the sideline during practice to tell me he was switching my race to the 4×400 relay. Anyone who knows track and field knows the huge difference between the 200-meter and the 4×400 relay. First off, running the 200 meters was just me against about ten other girls. My attitude was if I lost, I lost. I was only there to hang out and be social, you know, just having fun. But the 4×400 relay was like a team of four within a team of the track club. They depended on one another to win. When I saw the other girls the coach was expecting me to team up with, fear gripped me quickly. They were the girls who were never socializing. Those girls did all the drills correctly, and their times were always the fastest in their races. Unlike my friends and I, they were not there simply to have fun. They wanted to win, so they prepared to win. I wondered what it would take, aside from actually practicing the drills, for me to win too. After practice, I spoke with the relay team coach, and he made it plain and simple; I should:

1.  begin to eat properly and get enough sleep,
2.  wear the proper attire, and
3.  show up to practice on time with a heart for the race.

Many times, we put ourselves last in day-to-day life, jeopardizing our good health by eating badly and not getting enough rest. It was admirable on my part to make such drastic changes in my young lifestyle so that my teammates could continue to win. But I needed to know that I was important enough to make those lifestyle changes for myself too. You are important enough to this world to make lifestyle changes for yourself. But I'm telling you now it won't be easy.

My coach's words resonated with me throughout my life and became a standard by which I would try to live and teach my family.

*Begin to eat properly and get enough sleep.* You have heard countless numbers of times about the importance of eating properly and getting enough sleep. Well, here's one more time. I'm not a doctor, but I can tell you that getting the proper nutrition and adequate amounts of sleep makes a vast difference in the way I feel and the way my mind functions on a daily basis. In fact, your brain works hard to design your thoughts, feelings, breathing, and bodily movements, and food fuels your brain so that it is able to do all those things. The type of food you eat determines how you think, how you feel, how you move. Nutritional Psychology is a growing school of psychology that says there is a connection between the foods we eat and the way our brains function. Getting adequate amounts of sleep parallels with the foods we use to fuel our brains or what we eat.

The year my daughters started a new elementary school together, at the end of their day, they would get into the car stoked as they told me the events of their day. I asked question after question, and they took turns answering based on each of their experiences. One day, I asked about lunchtime and recess: who they sat with at lunchtime, how many other kids sat at the same table, if they shared their lunches with friends. They each grew quiet and forlorn. Oh boy! That was the question that changed the atmosphere in the car. The previous jovial responses became monosyllabic answers bathed in quivery, meek tones with heads hung low and eyes that were glued to the floor of the car. I didn't want to bombard them with many more questions, but after a couple of days of this, my curiosity got the best of me, so I asked what was wrong, thinking perhaps that they didn't enjoy lunchtime as well as other parts of their days.

The response was hilarious to me, but I noted right away they didn't think it was funny at all. They took turns telling me that at lunchtime the other kids made fun of the lunches I packed, and my girls said they wished they could have a "regular lunch." Again, I thought it was a little humorous. At home, we practiced healthy eating habits most of the time, and I wanted them to take those same habits to school and into their adult lives. You see, I had made a conscious effort to pack lunches I knew would serve their bodies well. And listen, I'm not saying we never eat our favorite cookies and chips. In fact, we eat them enjoyingly, but the key is that we don't partake of them on a regular basis. It's not our lifestyle. Paul writes in 1 Corinthians 10:31, "Whether then, you eat or drink or whatever you do, do all to the glory of God." This means everything you do should be done for God's glory, even eating and drinking.

*Wear the proper attire.* The way you dress and adorn your body is also an important part of running the race of life. This part is not about judgment and scorn. You know the adage "dress for success." Dress the part to be successful in whatever you're doing or aspiring to do. If you are aspiring to be a fashion designer, wear fashionable clothes, perhaps something you have designed yourself. If you want to work in a corporate setting, you wouldn't wear a dress you'd wear to the beach. Runners and people who exercise regularly wear light clothing that will keep the temperature of their bodies cool, so appropriately you may see more of their bodies.

We must remember that our mission is for others. We are to have such a profound impact on another individual that a shift in their thinking occurs, which causes a shift and transformation in their behavior. Can you think of a time when someone else's influence caused transformation in you? Or a time your influence did the same. As young women, dressing in a way that is indecorous or undignified brings negative attention to ourselves from others. I get it. It's difficult in this age of social media to find a role model who will not buy into the objectification of young girls, purporting that the more attention you receive, the more you are loved and, therefore, accepted. The culture will have you believe that you are defined by the measure of physical attractiveness you possess.

I like to think attractiveness is really measured by more than physical beauty. Consider these statements and questions that show attractiveness in character.

1. The degree to which you are brave and courageous in the face of adversity is alluring and attractive to others.
2. Are you comfortable standing alone on a decision you've made that goes against what the crowd has decided?
3. Does your presence in an atmosphere fill it with peace or contention?

*Show up to practice on time with a heart for the race.* The older I got, the more "show up to practice on time" took on a different meaning. In track and field, programming and practicing certain muscles of our bodies to perform in a way for optimal performance in a particular race is key to winning. Later in life it came to mean showing up for myself on a regular basis in whatever I was pursuing that was heartfelt to me. And I can't say initially I understood what "a heart for the race" meant. But it didn't take long for me to figure it out. I simply looked at my teammates, and their hearts for what they were doing shone brightly in everything they did from the moment they arrived at practice to the moment it was time to leave. They wore focus, determination, and grit on their faces like a shadow eclipsing the sun. You knew it was there because the atmosphere had shifted. When they practiced, the atmosphere shifted. I want to tell you to show up for your race and get excited about it. Get so excited about your race and what you are doing that when you walk into the room, the atmosphere shifts. If you think you may be in the wrong race, like I was, try another. There is no shame in not knowing what you were designed to do and how to go about doing it if you are seeking to find out.

Now, another important aspect of caring for your body is learning that the Holy Spirit resides in you the moment you decide to allow Him in. The very moment. The role of the Holy Spirit in our lives is to help us, so by all means, ask Him to come into your heart right away if you haven't already. I actually make a practice of inviting Him into my life on a daily basis. One of my favorite Bible verses of all time is Galatians 5:16. "Walk by the Spirit, and you will not carry out the desires of the flesh." Do you know how many times in a day I am reminded of this verse? A lot! At times my days are filled with such chaos and discord that I have to call on the Spirit as my helper; otherwise, my own desires will supersede, and I will find myself having to ask for forgiveness all day long. Thank God for the Holy Spirit alive in us.

> "Do you not know that your body is a temple of the Holy Spirit who is in you, whom you have from God, and that you are not your own?"
>
> 1 Corinthians 6:19

What this means is your body belongs to God to reside there in the form of the Holy Spirit, guiding you and helping you in all circumstances. You don't have to imagine help in the circumstances, trials, heartbreak, misfortune of your life. It's guaranteed because that is why the Holy Spirit is available to us. He advocates for us with the Father. You were bought with the price of Jesus' life, so why not honor God with your own life? Allow the Holy Spirit inside of you to be magnified. Think about the unspeakable love and adoration God has for you that He would provide you with an indwelling of Himself that guides you to Himself like a gift beautifully wrapped in truth, and you open it over and over whenever you need it, and it's always the truth of the matter. What a God you serve.

## Wearing Emeralds

Explain what you like most about your body, and then list three ways you plan to take care of it.

_____

_____

_____

_____

_____

_____

_____

_____

_____

_____

_____

_____

_____

_____

_____

_____

_____

_____

_____

## Word Power

Strong: *Effective or efficient, especially in a specified direction.*

Would you describe yourself as strong? Explain why you would or would not. Give an example of your answer.

_____

_____

_____

_____

_____

_____

_____

_____

_____

_____

_____

_____

_____

_____

_____

_____

_____

_____

_____

Pam Wilcox

For Alicia

*"God is developing you to prepare you for the future. Learn to be faith-ful, and He will open the doors for you."*

CHAPTER 3

# Your Gifts and Talents

*Gifted*

When my daughters were still being formed inside of me, I prayed to ask God that once they were born, He would reveal to me their gifts and talents. I wanted to ensure that my husband and I gave them everything they needed to nurture and cultivate their gifts. Dear Daughter, everyone, regardless of his belief in God, has natural abilities known to them as gifts and talents. Spiritual gifts are given to Christians to serve other believers in building the body of Christ by serving one another. In a later chapter, we'll talk more about spiritual gifts.

Gifts and talents, your natural abilities, are sometimes passed down to you from your parents or grandparents. Perhaps your mother is a gifted writer and speaker or singer or dancer. Then you can potentially be gifted to do those things as well. Some of you may have a natural inclination for music, art, math, running, writing, designing, and the list goes on. Sometimes your environment enhances your natural ability. If you witness your talented father practicing piano every day, you could possibly develop a talent for playing as well. Most importantly it is God Himself who endows you with natural gifts and talents. Amazing evidence of this is in Exodus 31:1–6 when God was speaking to Moses about the talents He bestowed upon Bezalel and Oholiab.

> The Lord said to Moses, "See, I have called by name Bezalel the son of Uri, son of Hur, of the tribe of Judah, and I have filled him with the Spirit of God, with the ability and intelligence, with the knowledge and all craftsmanship, to devise artistic designs, to work in gold, silver, and bronze, in cutting stones for setting, and in carving wood, to work in every craft. And behold I have appointed with him Oholiab, the son of Ahisamach from the tribe of Dan."
>
> Exodus 31:1–6

After the exodus of the children of Israel from Egypt, God wanted them to build a place where He could dwell among them, like a tabernacle. He chose a man by the name of Bezalel to oversee its construction. He was a very accomplished man, having talents that ranged from gem cutter to engraver, woodworker, jeweler, and metal worker. He was multitalented and was more than qualified to build the sanctuary God wanted.

God always equips us with those things we need to carry out a task he has before us.

Can you imagine being born with the ability to do something so well that you're nearly an expert at it? Can you? Can you believe that God loves you so much that He created you with this thing that you not only do exceptionally well, but you love doing? It interests you, excites you, and you want to talk about it or do it all the time. Here's the caveat. If you do not use your gifts, you will lose your gifts. It's like anything sitting on a shelf that's never been used. It begins to collect dust in the cracks and crevices of its core, and the dust is so thick that it causes a malfunction in the item if you suddenly try to use it. Just like your very own gifts and talents. Your gifts and talents should be cultivated, nurtured, and practiced. Remember you are not cultivating, nurturing, and practicing your gift for yourself. You are doing it to bring glory to God. When you don't use your gifts and talents, you are literally telling God you don't want them.

I remember the very moment God revealed one of Kierstin's gifts and talents to me and her dad as being very blatant and naked with the truth. She was turning eight years old, and Kerrigan was a smart, savvy four-year-old. Kierstin's new school required all grade levels to participate in the Academy of Christian Schools International Speech Meet Competition each year. It was so fun watching Kierstin prepare for the competition as she recited a poem entitled "What Makes a Teacher." Even Kerrigan got involved pretending to be her audience many nights after dinner, intently listening. Being our first time at the school we had no idea what to expect from this competition and thought it was so cute that Kierstin was participating and was trying very hard. However, on the day of the competition, when her name was called, she took center stage, and the seven-year-old I saw on stage was confident, brave, and without reserve as her voice radiated through the huge auditorium filled with hundreds of spectators. My husband and I looked at one another, and we cried because we knew that clearly and without a doubt she was indwelled by God with the ability to captivate an audience with her voice. We knew that when the winners were announced, she would be one of them. She was. We found out that day that one of her gifts was public speaking! The confirmation of this gift to speak well and affect her audience was not just Kierstin receiving first place among hundreds of other second graders but that she received first place year after year after year. She went on for the next three years to win first place in all of ACSI until she left that school. She did! What's more interesting about that is public speaking is one of Kerrigan's gifts and talents too. When Kierstin took center stage for the first time, Kerrigan sat between my husband and me, reciting the same speech Kierstin was reciting on stage! She had listened to Kierstin practice so much that she was learning it too, word for word! We cried doubly from laughter and shock! God is the amazing Giver of all things, all things. It was simply amazing that, because every day after school Kerrigan and I watched Kierstin practice her poem for the Speech Meet Competition, she, at three and a half years old, had, in fact, learned it as well!

And here's another interesting fact. Neither one of the two is currently pursuing anything to do with public speaking! Sometimes God indwells us with gifts and talents for a season of our lives, but other times those same things will be revisited in our futures. The key is to always be seeking in the moment what you are supposed to be doing for that moment.

Your gifts and talents say you have a unique mission on earth that God has ordained only you to carry out. Everything you need to do is God's will He gave to you in your gifts. As you grow into the young woman God wants you to be, there will inevitably be trials along the way, doors closed in your faces, and rocks you will stumble over. But if you are walking in your gifts and talents, you will be victorious in all trials, windows will open, and the rocks you stumble over will not cause you to fall! So go for it! When you are "going for it," remember Romans 8:37: "For in all things we overwhelmingly conquer through Him who loved us."

You can easily identify what your gifts and talents are. Here are five ways:

1. You are passionate about doing it.
2. It comes naturally to you. You barely have to try to do it.
3. You always get compliments from other people about it, even strangers.
4. You will inevitably experience success doing it.
5. At least one family member, your parents or grandparents especially, are gifted in the same area.

First of all, you are passionate about whatever you are gifted and talented at doing. You love doing it and share excitement about it with those around you. Your passion for it leads you to constantly talk about it. If you could, you would want to do this thing every day and all day. What are you passionate about?

With little effort and without even trying, you start out being better than your peers who may be doing the same thing.

You'll find that people who are closest to you are surprised to learn that you are really good at doing this thing and may think it just came out of nowhere when, in all actuality, the season for its manifestation hadn't come into fruition yet. They will constantly say how good you are and may even help you to cultivate it.

Any time there is purposeful intentionality activating your gifts and talents, your success is guaranteed. There are two major reasons why. The foremost reason is because God says so throughout the Bible. In Proverbs 14:23 God inspired the richest man who ever lived, King Solomon, to instruct us, "In all labor there is profit but mere talk leads only to poverty." Proverbs 22:29, "Do you see a man skilled in his works? He will stand before kings; He will not stand before obscure men." Proverbs 21:5, "The plans of the diligent lead surely to advantage." And there are countless other verses that say success is the result of using our gifts and talents diligently. The second reason your success is guaranteed relates wholly to diligence and your gifts and talents. It's simple: when something is done over and over, what's actually happening and is occurring is a perfecting of the skill.

Ever heard of the 10,000-hour rule? The concept was first coined by a Swedish psychologist who stated that in order for a level of expertise in a certain area to occur, it must be practiced for 10,000 hours. I first came across the concept in author Malcolm Gladwell's book *Outliers*.[2]

Lastly, can you think of a family member who is really good at something you're gifted to do as well? We are the product of our environment and our genes, as they relate to our giftings.

I think if you were to do an ancestry test delving back five, six, or seven generations, you would find someone in your lineage was talented in something you do.

Girl, you should be excited to use your gifts and talents. What an exciting realization to know that if you use your gifts and talents, you will be so successful that important people of great stature will know who you are. They will not only know who you are, but they will seek to help you in your area of expertise. You will begin to see doors you thought were shut open. When you use your gifts and talents to do what God has ordained you to do, you will gain favor with people of influence. How exciting is that? To know that God will bless your gifts and talents so much so, He will use powerful people to further your agenda, which is really His agenda. Remember He gifts you with expertise in an area to bless others in His name.

What do you think the world would look like if everyone knew what their gifts and talents were? Furthermore, what would it look like if everyone used their gifts and talents to do good in the world? That's what I want to encourage you to do. You are gifted. You are talented. You are this extraordinary young lady with worth, possessing more than you know. It's time for you to know your worth and walk into spaces with the confidence and bravery that is yours. It's time for you to possess the land. Your land.

When you decide to take your gifts into this world, you will see how this will inspire other girls your age to do the same. They will want to be just like you. They will wonder how you became so successful, and you'll be able to explain your journey of self-discovery, motivating them to do the same. What are you waiting for? Start identifying and embracing your gifts and talents now. The next section, "Wearing Emeralds," will help you to do so.

## Wearing Emeralds

List those things you believe are your gifts and talents. What are you passionate about? What do you do exceptionally well? It can be more than one thing. Think of your parents and grandparents' gifts and talents and list something you are similarly gifted to do. After you have listed your gifts, write a plan on how you will use them to bring honor to God.

_____

_____

_____

_____

_____

_____

_____

_____

_____

_____

_____

_____

_____

_____

_____

_____

_____

_____

_____

## Word Power

Gifted: *Having exceptional talent or natural ability.*

What do you do that requires little or no effort and you do it really well? Do you dream of doing this as a profession later in life?

_____

_____

_____

_____

_____

_____

_____

_____

_____

_____

_____

_____

_____

_____

_____

_____

_____

_____

Alison Edelere-Gordon
For Zayna

*"A dream is a precious gift. It is an image of what we can do when we
suspend inhibitions. Capture them, fiercely protect them, and then
live life as the beloved child of a father who makes dreams come true."*

## CHAPTER 4

# Your Hopes and Dreams

*Dreamer*

Dear Daughter, what are your hopes and dreams? In your
solitude, away from the noise of day-to-day life, what do you
hope for, and what do you dream about? How do you imagine
yourself in the future? The Bible defines hope as a confident
expectation (Romans 8:24–25 and Hebrews 11:1, Life Application Study Bible). Dreaming, in the context I am referring to, is
picturing yourself in the future. I'll define "hoping and dreaming" together as the picture of what you confidently expect your
future to look like when the culmination of your desires, which
should be rooted in God's plan for you, merge with God's destiny for your life.

In the previous chapter, you were introduced to the topic of
your gifts and talents. God is such a brilliant God. He created

you with gifts and talents but then bore a desire in your heart to hope and dream for your future, with your gifts and talents being the foundation and core of what you hope for and what you dream about. To clarify, while your hopes and dreams are different from your gifts and talents, the two do intersect. When your hopes and dreams are fueled by what you are gifted and talented to do, the traverse or intersection of the two causes a maturing of the time that was designed for your success in the area of your gifting.

What is the guaranteed way to ensure the intersection of your hopes and dreams and your gifts and talents?

1. Formulate a plan that outlines your goals for what you desire to do or who you desire to be. Arriving at the place where you are living your hopes and dreams is a journey that will require you to plan how you will get there. When you construct a plan for your dreams, you will begin to see the mighty hand of God opening doors for you that will take you by surprise. This plan should be written down in a journal or notebook. Do not treat the idea of journaling your plans with nonchalance. I think writing a plan enables a brain-to-heart connection, and once something is in our hearts, we have a burning desire to birth it.

2. Outline what things you need to do to accomplish your goals. Be diligent in whatever practices you have determined will ensure you accomplish those goals. Diligence is key for the success of anything you will do.

3. Refer back to your plan often. Sometimes our plans need adjusting before we can successfully accomplish a goal. This is why it is imperative to refer often to the plan. You may even find that your plan changes as you grow from one stage of your life to another. Don't panic—this only means your hopes and dreams are evolving, and that's wonderful. Nothing is set in stone. What you hope for today may be completely different than what you dream about tomorrow. That's okay—it's normal, in fact. All of it will bring immeasurable joy to you.

The Bible says in Romans 15:13, "Now may the God of hope fill you with all joy and peace in believing, so that you will abound in hope by the power of the Holy Spirit."

I assure you when you bridge your hopes and dreams to the foundation of God's Word, you can expect that He will bring you to the place where you are living out what you hope for and what you dream about.

"Commit your work to the LORD, and your plans will be established" (Proverbs 16:3).

As you get older, God may place even more hopes and dreams in your heart in addition to the ones already there. That's the beauty of growing in your relationship with the Father and growing as a person. You are forever evolving.

Now, take a moment to look at the diagram below. I call it the Clock of Hopes and Dreams. This concept is based solely on the experiences of seeing my own daughters' hopes and dreams and noting the stages of life they were at and the ages they were. It's to help you understand the hopes and dreams in your heart and how to process them at each stage of your development. Even look back and recall if, in fact, you yourself experienced these same things as you were growing up. The Clock of Hopes and Dreams says anywhere from birth to the age of thirteen you are becoming acquainted with what you like and dislike. You want to play around with your interests, and it consumes your time. Once you are a little older, around the ages of thirteen to fifteen, you've given up some things and held others close. Those things you've held close, you visualize yourself doing in the future. You begin to dream and set goals based on those dreams. Once you are about fifteen to eighteen years old, you are seriously thinking about your future and formulating a mental picture to reach the goals you have set. Lastly, at the age of around eighteen and beyond, you are purposefully working to make your dreams a reality. It could be at this time you are preparing for college or a career. You know that it will take time, hard work, and commitment to a carefully thought-out plan to someday live in your hopes and dreams as you utilize the gifts and talents you have. You are satisfied and feel a measure of comfort and excitement at the fact that you can possibly attain your hopes and dreams. You are enjoying the journey and embracing the process.

Interestingly, for every new hope or dream as you are growing in age as well as in maturity, this clock is reset, and the circle begins again. Let's say you were given a soccer ball as a gift for your fifth birthday. You play with that ball all the time and coincidentally see soccer being played on television at the age of twelve. You continue to enjoy playing soccer, now on an organized team; the difference is you begin to want to do it even more. Others notice you are a notch above other soccer players on your team; your skill in the game is more advanced than others. Once you are around the age of fifteen, you begin to dream of playing soccer in college. You know that getting there takes hard work, and you evaluate whether you are serious enough to set goals based on your vision for playing in college. Perhaps you can go into your backyard and dribble the soccer ball for thirty minutes a day. Maybe you can join a team that will challenge you to be better than you are. How about trying out for the high school team?

Fast forward a few years. Now you are actually in college playing soccer; you have reached your goal. You are so happy that you are singing about it in the shower of your dorm room. Your roommate hears you and thinks you have a phenomenal voice, so she invites you to meet her father, who is a music producer. Her father thinks with training you could actually record an album. You now have a new goal, and your Clock of Hopes and Dreams is reset! (Oh, the power of imagination... and dreaming!)

This Clock of Hopes and Dreams is what typically happens in the process of hoping and dreaming about your future as you utilize your gifts and talents. Again, based on my experience with my own two daughters, watching them grow and listening to the things of their hearts, I was able to construct this diagram with the corresponding age milestones. This diagram is used only to help you understand that process if you are already on this path. It is not designed as a prerequisite to accomplishing your hopes and dreams. It's simply the things I noticed at certain ages in my own daughters' development that made me believe they were consistently thinking about what they wanted to be in life at older ages. Our conversations during those times helped me to identify what my daughters were good at doing and if we should pursue lessons in those areas. I'll bet if you were to ask your own mother to tell you about conversations you and she had about your dreams, she would tell you things that you and she talked about that interested you and perhaps you currently do now.

My younger daughter appeared downstairs one day, eight years old, enthusiastically explaining how one day she was going to be a singer and record albums that everyone would buy. She started a YouTube channel where she would post herself singing and playing the piano. Today, she's a sophomore in college hoping to obtain a degree in environmental law. But she's gifted to sing, play the piano, and write. But she is guided by her own plan, bathed in who God says she is. Who am I to tell her to do something contrary to what's in her heart? What she is gifted and talented to do. Perhaps someday it will all come full circle.

Girl, your hopes and dreams are planted inside of you by God, and He intends for you to fully hope and dream without fear.

Age 5-13
Theres Passion in Your Heart
for Things You Love to Do

Age 13-15
What Goals Will
You Set to Develop
Your Passions

Age 18-21
Establishing a
Plan and Setting
New Goals

Clock of Hopes and Dreams

Age 15-18
Assess Whether Your Passions are Changing

## Wearing Emeralds

Glance at the Clock of Hopes and Dreams and identify the hopes and dreams in your heart, set some goals, and write your plan. Use this diagram to identify where you are on your journey.

_____

_____

_____

_____

_____

_____

_____

_____

_____

_____

_____

_____

_____

_____

_____

_____

_____

_____

_____

## Word Power

Hope: *To want something to happen or be the case.*

Dream: *A cherished aspiration, ambition, or ideal.*

Use the space below to talk about your hopes and dreams. Have your hopes and dreams changed as you've grown older?

_____

_____

_____

_____

_____

_____

_____

_____

_____

_____

_____

_____

_____

_____

_____

_____

_____

_____

_____

_____

Lisa Burdick

For Lauren and Kristen

*"Your friendships are your garden. Nourish each friendship with the love and care that each one requires. With a servant's heart, plant the seeds of your time, unconditional love, support, trust, faithfulness, forgiveness, and the word of truth. And through the test of time, you will cultivate the most beautiful bouquet of friends whose uniqueness and purpose were perfectly designed by God to be such a gift to you. God sees us just the same when the wind blows, when the storms come, and when the sun shines so bright. So continue to seek the beauty in your garden every season."*

# CHAPTER 5

# Your Friendships

*Affable*

Dear Daughter, When I think of the word *friendship*, I immediately think of women and girls and how we are notorious for engaging in time spent with other females. I think our friendships are deeper than men's and boys' friendships because we like to invest our time and ourselves. We share things men don't; we bond over more things. We take the time to abide over a cup of tea, coffee, dinner, or lunch. We loan and borrow personal items like clothes, shoes, and jewelry. We exchange ideas about meal prep, hair tips, and recommendations on the best goods and services. Do men do that? No! Not like we girls do. And the value in doing these things is that it causes us to bond! I don't know about you, but I love being a girl. Love, love, love it.

But what sets our friendships most apart from those of men is that we have an innate urge, a need almost, to express our feelings to our female friends. We are authentic and raw about what is in our hearts and minds. Women are less afraid to be vulnerable and transparent with female friends. And I'm not saying we're closer to God than men are; I would never believe that. Nor am I saying God is a woman; that is utter nonsense. But what parallels do you notice in our relationships with other women and our relationship with God? We feel no reluctance or feelings of inadequacy about talking to Him. Telling Him our business. That same comfort we have with our female friends, we have it with God.

Girl, friends are a wonderful addition to your life. They are purposed to be a blessing to you by enhancing your life. God loved us so much that He designed friendship to be a clear representation of what He Himself looks like: love, kindness, mercy, grace, honesty, and forgiveness. And our friendships don't solely have to be with other females. You can enjoy the best of connections with males as well.

The Bible is laden with examples of beautiful friendships. One of the most exquisite examples of friendship in the Bible is that of Naomi and Ruth. When Naomi's husband and two sons die, she urges her daughters-in-law, Ruth and Orpah, to return to their families as she had planned to return to her homeland, Bethlehem, after her family had settled in Moab to escape a famine in Judah. These two Moabite daughters-in-law chose differently. Orpah hearkened to Naomi's wishes, but Ruth wanted direly to remain with Naomi, so she did. That was the beginning of one of the most admired friendships of all time. I urge you to take some time to read the story of this sweet and endearing friendship. Aside from many other things, this relationship teaches us three things:

1. *Friendship is giving.* Ruth gave of herself to live life alongside Naomi. She was in service to Naomi, perhaps because she felt an everlasting bond having been married to Naomi's son.
2. *Friendship knows no lines of demarcation.* Naomi was much older than Ruth. Ruth was a Moabite, and Naomi was an Israelite.
3. *Friendship should have a foundation rooted in love for the Father.* Ruth began to serve Naomi's God. The one true God.

Another endearing friendship in the Bible is that of David and Saul's son Jonathan. David's and Jonathan's relationship is one of the most amazing and deepest friendships recorded in the Bible. The Bible demonstrates for us how they put their commitment to God in the middle of the friendship. When their friendship became tested, they grew closer together instead of allowing the vices of the enemy to destroy it. Jonathan was the prince of Israel but realized he would not be the next king but that David would be instead. Jonathan chose to lose the throne to his best friend than to lose his best friend to the throne. But the loving-kindness Saul, Jonathan's father, had felt for David began to turn into jealousy. When Saul pursued David to kill him, Jonathan stood by his friend. You can read the story of their friendship in 1 Samuel chapters 18–20. It's truly extraordinary!

One of the most important parts of the dynamic of friendship is if you want true friends, you must show yourself to be a true friend as well.

Friendship is an important part of your life, as the influence of friends runs deep into the fabric of your own character. The influence is subtle and evasive but sure. As you choose your friends, remember who you become friends with now has a lifelong effect on your future, and that effect could be positive, enlightening, and pure or negative, yielding dire consequences.

> "Do not be deceived: 'Bad company corrupts good morals.'"
> 1 Corinthians 15:33

Choose your friends wisely and carefully. Ask God to plant wonderful friends in your life and remove those whose values and hearts don't align with who He is. I've asked God that very thing for my own life, and over the years I've seen bonds broken with individuals I've considered friends, and not once did I regret ending the relationship. Don't be afraid to close a door on friendships that bring no value to your life. You will know when it's time to end a relationship because God will show you.

Just recently, I had to end a friendship of nearly fifteen years, and surprisingly it wasn't very hard. There were no ifs, ands, or buts about what I needed to do. Hopefully you will never need to end a friendship because all of your friends will seek to provide a foundation of love and care. But...if you do, there are two degrees to which you can do this. You will know which one suits your situation best.

1.  Set boundaries—setting boundaries is not really ending the friendship. It's really redefining it. And you redefine it when the friendship is not serving you the way it once has, but you still want to occasionally engage in relationship with the individual. This person is not intentionally harming you, but his or her actions do cause you to think about whether you can continue to grow with them constantly in your atmosphere.
2.  Cold turkey end it! Completely sever ties because those ties have become a noose around your neck. The main reason for ending the friendship is that this person is causing your spiritual growth to be stunted. This person is hindering blessings from God. Literally.

The friendship of fifteen years I ended was cold turkey. Send a text, write a letter, make a phone call, but do it after praying for guidance. I chose to write my friend a letter thanking her for her friendship but afterward set boundaries designating my choice to end the friendship. This girl was stunting my ability to reach spiritual maturity because every time I was around her, she was mean-spirited toward me. Her tongue was a hotbed of insults and degradative language. My husband and I knew the root cause of the animus but felt I shouldn't be subjected to meanness because of her unhappiness with her personal life. So we decided as a family to end the relationship. I will tell you, when we did, it was like a heaviness dropped from my heart and God filled it with such joy and peace that I began to weep. And guess what else God did? He replaced that space with thirty new friends! Thirty! I am not exaggerating! So go and be courageous if you need to end a friendship. He will be with you, and you will begin to bask in the freedom God always intended.

Friends encourage, guide, motivate, empathize, and hold you up. Literally. Much like Aaron and Hur held up Moses' arms during a battle because each time Moses lowered his arms because he grew tired, the Amalekites began to prevail against Moses and the Israelites. But when he raised his arms, the Amalekites began to lose. So the Bible tells us in Exodus 17:11–12 Aaron and Hur brought a stone for Moses to sit on, then positioned themselves to hold up Moses' arms!

Who is holding up your arms? Who is positioning themselves and deciding that no matter how long it takes, they are going to hold up your arms because they know you are tired from a battle you are fighting? Whose arms are you holding up?

True friends won't ask you to break rules or laws. True friends won't expect you to abandon your values and morals for friendship. A friend will never stand in judgment of who you are, defining and attributing your shortcomings to you being a bad person and, therefore, you not being worthy of their friendship. Never!

For a while it can be a lonely place to stand firm in your belief system. But I promise you that if you persevere and cry out to the Almighty Father, He will bring into your life the perfect relationships in girls and boys just like you. Those who refuse to compromise their beliefs and futures to be friends with someone who doesn't honor God, someone who chooses the things of this world.

Certainly, I am not suggesting to not befriend people who don't know God. That, too, is absurd. But what I am saying is because non-Christians do not base their lives on what God says on a matter, we as Christians should not allow their influence in the matters of our own lives. I have a myriad of friends who are not Christians, and we enjoy good friendships. They give great advice and support in time of need. They are giving, empathetic, kindhearted, and smart. They love hard and give grace when needed. They are wonderful friends to me and my family.

What do healthy friendships look like? It's the person whose friendship you find easy, supportive, and reliable that is most valuable to you. It's just like God's love for you: easy in that it's unconditional, reliable because it's always there no matter what, and valuable because it's as rare as the world's most sought-after gem. There's no love like it! John 3:16 said it best. "For God so loved the world that He gave His only begotten son, so that whosoever believes in Him should not perish but will have everlasting life."

Who is your absolute best friend? Jesus. John 15:12–15 says:

> This is My commandment, that you love one another, just as I have loved you. Greater love has no one than this, that one lay down his life for his friends. You are my friends if you do what I command you. No longer do I call you slaves, for the slave does not know what his master is do-

ing; but I have called you friends, for all things that I have heard from My Father I have made known to you.

He valued you so much that He gave His life for you. Who else, outside of your parents, do you know would give their lives for you? Very few people I'm sure. Jesus really is your absolute best friend. You and He are friends above your friendships with others. Spend time with Him, hang out with Him, ask His advice on matters of your life, and take Him everywhere you go. Laugh with Him, cry with Him, have fun with Him, and share your life with Him. He's waiting for you.

## Wearing Emeralds

Take a moment to make a list of all the people you consider close friends. Then list their qualities and characteristics—the good and the bad. What value do they bring to your life? Ask yourself, "Is Jesus pleased with my friendship with this person?"

_____

_____

_____

_____

_____

_____

_____

_____

_____

_____

_____

_____

_____

_____

_____

_____

_____

_____

## Word Power

Affable: *Friendly, good-natured, or easy to talk to.*

What are the characteristics you look for when choosing your friends? Do you believe you possess these same character traits?

_____

_____

_____

_____

_____

_____

_____

_____

_____

_____

_____

_____

_____

_____

_____

_____

_____

Courtney Williams
For Jamie

*"Your feelings are valid, but sometimes your thoughts are lies. You're not much and not enough. The devil's voice has gotten loud in your head. Shut him up, open your Bible, and remind yourself who God is and who He says you are."*

CHAPTER 6

# Your Fears

*Fearless*

Girl, fear is very real. It's actually a normal emotion to feel. In fact, many people aren't aware that fear can be healthy and fear can be unhealthy. You read that correctly. I know what you're thinking. That every time you've been afraid, it did not feel good. It made you morph into something other than yourself, rendering you helpless in your thoughts and mind. I know. Let's talk first about when fear is healthy.

Fear is healthy when there is an awestruck reverence for God, acknowledging His power and authority over everything in the world and over our lives. Proverbs 1:7 states, "The fear of the Lord is the beginning of knowledge." This verse may seem the reverse of what you think you should feel about God. He is a loving, amazing God that never does anything to hurt us. Why should you fear Him, and why is it healthy to fear God? Again, fearing God is the ultimate show of respect for Him and His majesty, His position, His character, and His being. It is, in a sense, bowing our lives to Him as He sits on the throne of life. The fear of God is respect for who He is. That's a healthy fear.

Unhealthy fear is the type of fear most of us feel. It, too, is connected to God because unhealthy fear is when our trust, hope, and faith in Him are unreachable, becoming nonexistent. This lack of trust in God when we experience challenges leads to a gamut of other debilitating things that can attack our minds, like sadness, depression, and anxiety.

Everyone experiences unhealthy fear at some point in their lives and many times over. The problem with unhealthy fear is that, if it is not addressed, it can become mentally paralyzing, and as a result, your life will be paralyzed as well. You cannot wish fear away when you are faced with an enemy whose goal is to destroy you—to completely take you out! You cannot wish fear away! You have to be purposeful in choosing not to be afraid. I get it. Sometimes that's hard because choosing not to be afraid requires exponentially more than just saying to yourself, "Don't be afraid." It involves empowering yourself with the tools to combat fear *before* you become fearful so that when you are attacked, you have a solution at hand. What are those tools?

1. Pinpoint the source of the fear. The ability and mindset to dissect the source of fear is asking yourself, "Why does this cause me to be afraid?" Typically, we become afraid when we think an outcome we need won't happen.

2. Train your brain not to catastrophize! According to the *Merriam-Webster Dictionary*, catastrophizing is a cogni-

tive distortion that involves imagining or believing that the worst possible outcome of a situation or event is the most likely or certain one even when there is no evidence to support it. It makes a problem seem more serious than it is.

3. Encourage yourself by opening your Bible and finding every scripture on combatting fear and meditating on them day and night. Memorize them so that when the attacks of your mind occur, you can attack back with the solidified, tried, and true word of God. As you do, tell the Father that your only hope for success and victory in your situation is solely in Him. That's faith.

Sometimes you are not even aware of those things that make you fearful. When is someone not aware of their fear? When trusting in God is difficult for you to do because you don't believe He is able to be victorious on your behalf. You feel the problem or issue is too big for even Him to resolve. A fear so great rises in you, and peace you have enjoyed in the past is gone! When you are living in fear on a daily basis, it becomes a part of your character, and you then begin to live fearfully, never experiencing the victory of God. Nor can you allow fear to grow or fester. Oh, but the good news is our amazing God is waiting for you to give Him your fear.

> "Do not fear, for I am with you; Do not anxiously look about you, for I am your God. I will strengthen you, surely I will help you, surely I will uphold you with my righteous right hand."
>
> Isaiah 41:10

Remember you now have powerful weapons in your arsenal against fear: the Word of God and faith. The Bible is the infallible, inerrant, comforting word of God given to you to arm yourselves to live victoriously here on earth. God repeatedly tells us He will never leave us alone to fight on our own. How will you contribute to changing the world if you are fearful?

It was Friday. We were enjoying family time during a snow day. We had been snowed in for three days and loved the break it gave us. Of course, a "snow day" in Dallas is more like a "there's ice on the ground that we wish was real snow, and because Texans don't know how to drive in ice, the city is shutting down" day. So we four were snuggled together in blanket after blanket on the sofa watching movie after movie and eating bad snacks and drinking hot chocolate. Someone's foot was on another one's stomach. Another's head was on someone's lap. An elbow was on another's leg. You get it—the space on the sofa was tight! So, when I leaned my elbow on the arm of the sofa to prop up my head with my hand under my chin, I felt them: two lumps, one on each side underneath my chin. They were hard and big but not painful. The fear gripped me immediately! How long had they been there? Long! They were huge, so obviously, they had been growing for a while!

When I told my husband, he became quiet, and I could see in his otherwise strong face him searching for the right words to say—words that would comfort me—but in that moment, they never came. Normally, he is the one who is the encourager, and my daughters and I look to him for the calm and peace some situations require. Normally, he disregards the attacks of the enemy immediately and crushes his head with the Word of God. Normally, he is our voice of reason. When he looked at me in that moment, I saw clothed on his face anxiety, as if it belonged there. He said, "Let's call the doctor."

After calling the doctor, he told us we would need to wait until the following Monday for an appointment. Girl! It was a Friday! And I was supposed to go an entire weekend with a battle going on in my mind?

That weekend was the longest weekend of my life. The first night I tossed and turned with thoughts that took me to places in my mind that were hopeless. It seemed the moment I found those lumps, every commercial on television was about cancer. When I picked up a magazine to read, there was an article listing the signs of some type of cancer. You see, those commercials and magazine articles did not coincidentally come to my attention. The enemy had lined them up for that moment to instill fear so great in me that my faith and peace would be shattered. There are no coincidences. The enemy wanted me to be afraid and to operate in that fear. So I spent countless hours that weekend on the internet (which I don't recommend doing) researching lumps in the body and countless other lumps-related topics. None of the information was encouraging or hopeful. In fact, it was downright dismal. That first night I began to feel the fear consuming my mind. But the second night, I decided to wake up the warrior girl in me—the one that uses the Word of God as her sword and buckler. What warrior girl did next became a roadmap for the times she would become fearful in the future. She whipped out her Bible and found every scripture on overcoming fear and healing. She then wrote each one of the scriptures on an index card and put each one on the headboard of her bed. As she lay in bed that night, she meditated on the scriptures over and over. The one that says, "But He was pierced through for our transgressions. He was crushed for our iniquities; The chastening for our well being fell upon Him, and by His scourging we are healed" (Isaiah 53:5). And the one that says, "The Lord will sustain him upon his sickbed; In his illness, You will restore him to health" (Psalm 41:3). And the one that says, "Then your light will break forth like the dawn, and your recovery will speedily spring forth, and your righteousness will go before you, The glory of the LORD will be your rear guard" (Isaiah 58:8). That night and every night thereafter warrior girl slept like a baby! And I was like, "Warrior girl, what took you so long to get here!"

When the doctor's examination revealed the tumors were actually noncancerous swollen salivary glands, my husband and I praised God right there in the doctor's office!

Girls, when you are fearful about anything, awaken your warrior girl and run quickly to the Word of God! When you read it with expectancy and meditate on it in quiet perseverance, you will feel the fear leave your heart and mind and be replaced with peace and faith. You will. Faith and fear cannot inhabit the same place. It's one or the other. I choose faith. And I know that's easier said than done, but what you'll need to do is find that thing, that process that will help you to stand in faith over your fear. For me it was declaring scriptures of good health and healing over myself. What was actually happening was me changing my thoughts to ones that were empowering and not debilitating.

Many times, you will find that you will need to encourage yourself. Your ability to do that is creating a relationship with yourself that builds the confidence you need to stand firm in the face of adversity. At the core of a successful relationship with yourself is the ability to protect your mind against negative, self-debilitating thoughts.

God wants you to have peace, the kind that when you are in the midst of a storm, you are not worried or afraid because you know God is in control of everything, and when you cry out to Him, He hears and cares and defends you!

When you begin to identify fear in your life, that is the beginning of your victory over it. I challenge you to believe that God will take your fear and cast it to the depths of a place so deep that the fear cannot escape there. Don't you see? One of the enemy's weapons against you is to instill a sense of fear so great in you that you cannot move forward in your design. The enemy's earthly agenda is to destroy you by any means necessary. But our God is an awesome God. He loves us so dearly, so sweetly, and so completely that for everything the enemy attacks us with, God gives us a tool to overcome, to win—that's the Bible.

Where is yours?

## Wearing Emeralds

What are you afraid of? Open your Bible and find every scripture on overcoming fear. Meditate on those scriptures day and night, and you will begin to walk in your freedom from fear.

_____

_____

_____

_____

_____

_____

_____

_____

_____

_____

_____

_____

_____

_____

_____

_____

_____

_____

_____

_____

## Word Power

Fearless: *Free from fear, brave.*

Describe a time your fear prevented you from doing something that was either required of you or desired by you.

_____

_____

_____

_____

_____

_____

_____

_____

_____

_____

_____

_____

_____

_____

_____

_____

_____

_____

_____

Anabela Galvao-Williams

For Natalia

*"Treat your relationship with your parents as your most valuable treasure on earth. That bond is so great and so fulfilling; it is truly priceless."*

## CHAPTER 7

# Your Parents

*Priceless*

Dear Daughters, let's talk about your parents and the relationship you have with them as well as the one God wants you to have with them. First, my prayer for you is that the parents you have are the same parents God intended you to have, and they are enriching you with everything you need to be successful in life: love, guidance, instructing in God's truth, providing your needs, training you in God's ways, and preparing you for your future. If, for some reason, you do not have the loving parents God intended for you, we will pray together before "Wearing Emeralds" that God will send individuals into your life whom you can depend on as a parental figure. I do this because, as young women, there are certain character-building traits you need at certain junctures in your life that only a parent, mentor, or parental figure can give.

"Hear, my son, your father's instruction. And do not forsake your mother's teaching; indeed, they are a graceful wreath to your head, and ornaments about your neck."

Proverbs 1:8–9

The parent-child dynamic is one that God must have been smiling on the whole time He was creating it. It's much like the relationship we have with Him, the Father. When you were born, you were completely dependent upon your parents for everything. You trust and have complete faith in them. That's exactly how you should be with the heavenly Father now. Although the older you grow, the more your dependency on your parents for your physical well-being lessens, and your dependency on God for everything should grow, strengthen in fact. The shift from parental dependency to a godly dependency will happen naturally and over time. The Bible says as parents we are charged with teaching our children the truth about God's Word because it is the standard by which you are to live.

The ultimate act of love by your parent is to introduce biblical truths to you, and those truths should be the foundation of your heart, the place you call home, and your life. I can't remember a time I did not know God, being the daughter of a church pastor. For as long as I can remember, I have embraced God the Father and Jesus Christ as His Son. I enjoy a faith-filled relationship with God, depending solely on Him for my life and well-being, knowing that someday I will live in eternity with Him because I declare Jesus as my Lord and Savior. Knowing of God and being in relationship with God are two very different things, and oftentimes it is the parent who defines this distinction for the child.

The relationship of God as my Father and I as His child has changed many times over the years to culminate in a wonderful, beautiful realization that I no longer want to live without Him as my father, acquiring a respect for Him that surpasses the deepest desire of my heart, and knowing He is all I need. Getting to know the expectations He held for me wasn't always fun; in fact, it's been downright painful at times, mainly because I thought I knew what was best for my life better than He did. I lived in my feelings and often accused God of being too strict on me. But as I grew older, I began to experience Him, not merely know of Him. That's when everything changed! That's when I began to appreciate His love for me.

The parent-child relationship should be one of mutual respect, instruction, and a bond that will transcend peripheral influence. Daughter, embrace your parents' love and all that comes with it. Remember their birthdays, compliment their appearance, encourage their hopes and dreams (yes, we still hope, and we still dream), tell them you love them, value their opinions, and assure them that you place the love they have for you deep in your heart. Take the kisses they give, hold their hands, and initiate hugs. These are some of the things that strengthen the parent-child bond.

This may come as a surprise to you, but we know more than you give us credit for simply because we've already lived the life you are navigating now, so draw from our experiences. Girl, I know you are smart enough to realize we have a wealth of knowledge and information at your disposal!

Parents bring so much value to our lives. My own mother built my self-esteem single-handedly! Well, maybe Dad threw in a few things every now and then. As a young girl searching for who I was, wanting to know my place in the world, he complimented my dresses, told me he liked my hair, and always pulled out my chairs. I know the reason I expected those same things from the young men I dated was the result of my father's direct intention to teach me what I should expect from young men I dated.

There were so many wonderful moments when my mother encouraged me and dismantled my insecurities. One time in particular was as an eighteen-year-old. Hours before meeting my first boyfriend's parents, she and I were in the bathroom as she worked very diligently to do my hair knowing it would please me, the detail and care she took. With each stroke of the brush, the calm she possessed was transferred to me like a sweet blanket of security. But still, I was quietly imagining what the moment meeting them would bring. My mother allowed me the quiet until I said, "Mom, I hope they like me." I stared at her through the mirror we both stood in front of searching her face for her hope for me. She, too, used the mirror to look me in the eyes. Then she said, "You are amazing, beautiful, and intelligent. You should hope that you like them!" That was so long ago, and I feel the emotion of that moment as if it happened yesterday. After that moment, I remember trying to be amazing, beautiful, and intelligent even more. My mother taught me in that moment that I was worthy of love, worthy of someone liking me. Parents champion our causes and identify the priceless beauty we are as girls. My mother did. Here are some things that help to nurture the parent-child relationship:

1.  Always respect the position of authority that God has placed your parents in. Show respect at all times in the way you speak to them, your body language toward them, and your obedience to the direction and guidance they give.

2.  Parents should always provide you a safe place to express your emotions, and you should feel comfortable expecting this.

3.  Communicate, communicate, and communicate more. Never leave something in your heart or mind unsaid if it is a bridge to your parents understanding you better, therefore nurturing your relationship.

4.  Respect your parent's boundaries, and they should respect yours. Sometimes, as parents, we forget our daughters' personalities are evolving and they are hitting growth milestones, so the expectations we had when you were thirteen we're still trying to apply at seventeen. Ask for an adjustment that better represents your growth.

The bond created between a mother and child, a mother and daughter, begins at the moment of conception. It's there in the womb the mother is providing a safe place for you to grow, thrive, and develop. And while you are there in the womb, mothers are planning for your entry into the world. We are dreaming about you, hoping about you, and loving you even while you are there in the womb. All of this culminates in a powerful love.

The bond between you and your mother, first created there in her womb, evolves over time, and it is the responsibility of both the mother and daughter to protect that evolution. We must be careful that the bond is not broken. Yes, there will be times when the bond is tested because external factors influence relationships. But, girl, protect your relationship with your parents at every stage of the relationship.

Prayer for the daughter with no earthly parents: Father, thank You for this opportunity to pray for (please insert your name here) _____. Make the contents of this book come alive to her and the objective of its application be advanced beyond what she can imagine because the Holy Spirit will assure it. Please let her know holding this book in her hands and learning about You is no coincidence. But instead, it is the power of Your providence working on her behalf. You are mapping her path to You, and you are rooting for her to find You. Send into her life individuals who will adore her and embrace the idea of serving as her earthly parents. Make them her place of calm and familiarity here on earth, her place to learn more about You. Fill her life with Yourself so that she no longer feels an emptiness in her heart and life, yearning for earthly parents. God, if Your daughter is feeling any measure of emotions—sadness, fear, anxiety, or shame—that she does not have earthly parents, heal her so that her thoughts and feelings align with who You say You are to her. Remove the bondage that comes with these negative emotions so that the freedom You designed for her is rich with Your presence. Transform her life to make You the center, thereby gaining a father and mother whose love is unconditional, encompassing, and complete. In Jesus' name. Amen.

**Wearing Emeralds**

Write a letter to each of your parents expressing your gratitude for the constant they are in your life. If your parents are now in heaven, bury the letter as a time capsule near them or a place you have regular access to. If you have no earthly parents, write the letter to someone who has been like a parent to you.

Use the space below to write a copy of the letter you will bury and the name of the person you wrote your letter to.

_____

_____

_____

_____

_____

_____

_____

_____

_____

_____

_____

_____

_____

_____

_____

_____

_____

## Word Power

Priceless: *So precious that its value cannot be determined.*

Do you feel your relationship with your parents is priceless? Why or why not?

_____

_____

_____

_____

_____

_____

_____

_____

_____

_____

_____

_____

_____

_____

_____

_____

_____

_____

_____

Mitzi Willis, Esq.

For Taylor and Addison

*"No matter where you are, no matter what you do, there is nothing more important than your siblings, your family. You can have friends and seek shelter in their arms when things are tough at home, but the arms of your family are always open. Your siblings and family's love can never be replaced because family is priceless."*

# CHAPTER 8

# Your Siblings

*Devoted*

Dear Daughter, have you taken the time to really get to know your sisters and brothers? Are you purposeful in getting involved in one another's lives? It can be a wonderful experience to grow together with a sibling. The love that exists between siblings should be a natural love that is dependable, sure, and constant. Unfortunately, the very first sibling relationship is not a good example of a loving relationship. Cain killed his brother Abel. (I know what some of you are thinking! *Yes! Me too! I have wanted to kill at least one of my siblings when I was a child. But the jail time intimidated me!*) Many historians contend the root cause of the first murder in the Bible was anger, jealousy, and pride. Girl, discord among siblings is not a part of God's plan for the family. God's plan for siblings is much bigger than you know and is another remarkable way God's love for us is shown.

> "A friend loves at all times and a brother is born for a time of adversity."
>
> Proverbs 17:17

Friends are great to have as part of your life. But a sister or brother, a sibling, is who God placed in your life as a source of support. The Bible instructs us in Galatians 6:2 to "bear one another's burdens and thereby fulfill the law of Christ." Though this verse certainly applies to the sisters and brothers in Christ, together being His children, it also applies to the sibling relationship because aren't we, too, brothers and sisters in Christ?

He designed the sibling relationship as a place of solace we run to when we are broken, disheartened, or beaten up by the world. There, in that place of solace, you receive love, encouragement, solutions, and hope for your life. These are the same things God provides to us when we run to him broken. So, you see, you are to mirror to your siblings what God looks like, and they are to do the same for you. Sometimes God will do the sweetest thing in creating a bond so great between you and a friend that the friendship begins to evolve into a sibling-like relationship. This happens when you and your friend share things about yourselves and your lives that you feel comfortable trusting with each other. Your friendship is comfortable, you share things in common, you celebrate one another, and you can be yourself all the time without fear of judgment. When a friend becomes like a sibling, whether you know it or not, it's

God's handiwork providing you with something He knew you needed.

Be intentional in treating your sibling kindly, respectfully, and thoughtfully, investing the time and care it takes to nurture a loving siblingship. It's important to make the investment now, to strengthen the relationship now, because as you grow older, perhaps living hundreds of miles apart, you can draw from the relationship you shared earlier in life to maintain the one God intended and the one you desire. Time, coupled with many other influences, tends to change relationships. Maintaining the friendship between siblings requires work from all parties involved. Make phone calls, celebrate birthdays, commend achievements, and support ideas. What is the bottom line of cultivating a friendship as the basis of a sibling relationship? Being intentional.

I remember one Saturday afternoon I learned, from two little girls, a profound lesson in being intentional to show my siblings love. I found Kerrigan, my youngest, peering out the front window that faced the driveway leading to the *cul-de-sac* on which our house was built. I remember choosing that lot, especially for the reason of having the girls play there without concern for vehicular traffic. They often did as I often watched from the very window Kerrigan was now peering out. This particular Saturday afternoon was one of the most beautiful, sunny summer days we had experienced, as it was the beginning of summer, not yet sweltering hot. I had assumed Kerrigan was there, at the front window, smitten with the family of birds we had found nesting in the big tree just in front of the window days prior to this day. She had been so excited the day we found them and vowed to protect them from the large black birds, crows I now believe, often circling the cul-de-sac. I wasn't sure how she planned to do that, as she was only five years old and the wingspan on the crow was almost three feet! We often wondered why those crows were even there. My husband had rationalized that the crows had come from the nearby lake, along with the deer, coyotes, and other small rodents frequenting the neighborhood.

I noticed Kerrigan there at the window for about ten minutes until curiosity got the best of me, and I wanted to see what held her gaze for so long. When I approached Kerrigan and looked at her face, a single tear was rolling down her sweet cheek. Before I could speak, she looked up at me and pointed outside the window. I could see about twenty giggling girls jumping in anticipation, waiting in line for their turn to ride the pony on the edge of our driveway—a pony! Yes! On our driveway! Kerrigan had not been invited to the birthday party of the same-aged little girl next door. Oh, how she would have enjoyed a pony ride. She had never ridden a pony before, and to see some of the girls she knew from the neighborhood riding a pony and partially using our driveway to do it was hurtful and unbelievable. My mind raced to understand what was happening. By now several tears were streaming down Kerrigan's cheeks, and I wanted to burst.

Instead of bursting, we both turned to see Kierstin hopping toward us, her usual jovial self. Kerrigan looked up at her big sister, and when their eyes met, she pointed outside the window, tears still flowing.

She said, "Mom, can I go? I want to ride the pony too! Why didn't they tell me!"

Anger, hurt, confusion, and disbelief all toyed with my heart and head.

I said, "No." It was all I could gather with my broken heart. My beautiful little girls both learned a lesson about disappointment and sadness. We three stood there for a few seconds with our heartbrokenness, still watching little girls hopping up and down in anticipation of their turn to ride the pony. And they would be using our driveway! Did I mention that?

Then, as sure as the day was beautiful, a calmness swept across the room, and Kierstin bent down on her hands and knees and said, "Hey, Kerrigan, hop on! I'll give you pony rides!" Kerrigan climbed onto her sister's back, and she rode through the house giggling and having a sweet, precious moment with her big sister. It was like the breath of God breathed on the situation, and my little girl found her place of solace in my big girl! That's what siblings look like. That's what siblings do! They comfort one another and rescue one another with peace, joy, and pony rides.

And God's heart for us was even sweeter because we later received a huge apology from our neighbors about forgetting to invite Kerrigan. It relieved us to know that Kerrigan, indeed, would have been invited to the party where pony rides were the center of the cul-de-sac we shared with five other families. It relieved us to know that certainly, surely, for whatever reason another mother couldn't intentionally grieve the heart of a five-year-old who was a neighbor and in the same kindergarten class as her own daughter. It relieved us to know.

The most important thing I want you to get here is that because the first sibling relationship in the Bible resulted in the death of one of the brothers, the emotions felt by Cain before he enacted the murder of his brother are innate to all of us. What were those emotions Cain felt?

1. Envy—Cain wanted God to accept his offering, but God rejected Cain's offering and accepted Abel's instead.
2. Jealousy—Cain was afraid that because God accepted Abel's offering, Abel now possessed a favored standing with God, the standing Cain had as the firstborn son. The only reason we don't commit murder when we're angry with our siblings or anyone else is because we've learned, through practice, how to control our anger. Cain didn't.

Don't believe the societal lie that when siblings fight and don't get along—that it's normal. Sure, you will disagree with your siblings sometimes, and you will indeed fight. But to allow discord and animus to define your relationship is not what God intends. Discord in families is a vice of the enemy to ruin relationships and tear families apart. Be quick about resolving disagreements. Be open to working together to make peace that will always live in your family. Be willing to compromise and consider the other's position. When you do disagree or argue, touch, hug, embrace, rest your head on the other's shoulder. These are acts of humility, and those acts of humility really say, "I'm sorry," "I need you," "Let's start over."

Siblings are a gift from God, a sweet gift He provides to you as a measure of Himself. Protect the relationship with your siblings with every fabric of your being. You will find later in life that you are glad you did. If you and your siblings are not close, it's not too late for you to begin to forge a bond with them where God is the foundation. Plan to spend time working on your relationship with your siblings, and if you don't know where to begin, do so with a conversation letting your sibling know what you want in a relationship with him or her. Then watch the wonderful things God will unfold.

## Wearing Emeralds

List five things you will do to strengthen the bond between you and your siblings. Write a note or letter to your sibling. Use pencil and paper.

_____

_____

_____

_____

_____

_____

_____

_____

_____

_____

_____

_____

_____

_____

_____

_____

_____

_____

_____

## Word Power

Devoted: *Very loving or loyal.*

Explain how well you understand the degree to which God is devoted to you. Give the greatest example.

_____

_____

_____

_____

_____

_____

_____

_____

_____

_____

_____

_____

_____

_____

_____

_____

_____

_____

_____

Corbin Washington
For Trinity

*"My dearest daughter, I am so proud to be your mom. You are
strong and brave even when you think you are not. You push
through your pain and allow your beauty and your kindness to
radiate throughout your body. You, my love, are my hero."*

# CHAPTER 9

# Your Health

*Resilient*

Dear girl, you are so young and beautiful; embrace and celebrate the good health you are experiencing! A healthy body is God's plan for your life now and in the future because He wants you to live a long and healthy life. He designed your body perfectly so that you live fully and purposefully. Sweet, beautiful girl, if you are not in good health, don't despair. God knows exactly where you are on your journey to good health and gives you tools you need to get there: the expertise of doctors, medicine, food, and your determination. First, know that good health encompasses your body, mind, and spirit in totality. These three areas define the degree to which you are healthy, as together, they create the balance needed for total well-being. If one area of the balance is compromised or ill, then your good health is at risk: your body, your mind, and your spirit.

The World Health Organization defines health as "a state of complete physical, mental and social well-being and not merely the absence of disease or infirmity."

The physical: Your body is the beauty you see when you look into a mirror; your hair color, skin color, eye color, the shape of your lips, the length of your legs all define your body. Your internal organs and the care you take of them determine if your eyes will continue to glow, if your hair will grow healthily, if your skin will be blemish-free. Your body is resilient, so if you begin to commit to exercising it and filling it with healthy foods, you can restructure your body to its optimal health. How else can you go out into the world as warriors for the king if you are not managing your body well?

When there is a lack of exercise or unhealthy food choices on a continuous basis, it is a sure thing to expect that your body will let you know it is ill by weakening its immune system, causing you to then be susceptible to disease.

Sometimes we are predisposed to disease because of hereditary factors. Perhaps a parent has a disorder that has passed down to you because his or her parent had it as well. Whatever the case, it truly is your responsibility to journey to the restoration of good health. Remember the journey can be one of fulfillment, exploring ways to eat, exercise, and being intimate with God.

When we experience diseases and disorders that we will need to manage for the remainder of our lives, that can start out being difficult only because we haven't yet learned the tools we need to manage the disease. Even when you have a disease or disorder, you will need to manage the remainder of your life.

How you do that can bring a healthy balance to the disease. Here are some of the greatest tools you will need to empower yourself in managing your disease.

1.  Learn everything there is to know about the disease. This will arm you in knowing exactly how it will affect your day-to-day life.
2.  Gather a tremendous support system in our families, friends, and doctors.
3.  Join a support group. There are other girls with the same disease or disorder as you, and to be a part of a community in whatever you endure is God's gift to you and them.

The mental: Your mind is housed in your spirit and is where your thoughts originate. I know this is a difficult concept to understand, but Ephesians 4:23 refers to the "spirit of our minds." When you allow negative thoughts to drive your emotions, those emotions become negative, and negativity then has dominion over your body and can potentially cause illness. Yes! Your mind can cause your body to become ill! The research on the body/mind/spirit connection is astounding! The research also says that you can control what you allow to enter your mind by choosing what you will spend time thinking about. Turn a negative thought into a positive one by researching what the Word of God says about what you are thinking, and then allow your mind to think on what He says. Philippians 4:8 says, "Finally, brethren, whatever is true, whatever is honorable, whatever is right, whatever is pure, whatever is lovely, whatever is of good repute, if there is any excellence and if anything, worthy of praise, dwell on these things."

Your spirit is your thoughts and reactions driven by your emotions and also includes your attitudes, personality, and character. First Corinthians 2:11 asks, "For who among men knows the thoughts of a man except the spirit of the man which is in him? Even so the thoughts of God no one knows except the Spirit of God." All three aspects—body, mind, and spirit—that make you who you are need nurturing and care so the whole of you is healthy.

When a person is physically ill, it affects the whole person: body, mind, and spirit. The reverse of this is true as well. When a person is ill in mind and spirit, the body can be affected. Medical researchers say the three are interconnected and believe when one is not functioning at full capacity, the other two suffer as well. Many times, we can't see the negative effects sickness in our minds or spirits is wreaking on our bodies until it is too late. The sickness becomes manifest in the form of different diseases. Likewise, if our bodies are sick, we tend to allow our minds and spirits to become sick as well, in the form of negative thoughts and emotions. Think about it—when you have a minor cold or flu, do you physically feel like doing anything other than lying in bed? Do you begin to think a lot about all the unhappy things in your life—perhaps even becoming sad? Stress, sadness, anxiety, lack of joy and happiness, anger, and myriad other negative emotions can cause physical illness. Doctors have long said sickness is the result of disharmony of the body, mind, and spirit connection along with unhealthy eating and the lack of exercise. Perhaps our modern-day doctors were referring to what King Solomon said on the matter.

"A joyful heart is good medicine, but a broken spirit dries up the bones."

Proverbs 17:22

Maybe God created you without sight or hearing or missing a limb. This does not mean you are unhealthy. It means you were created like everyone else. Different. You are still beautiful and bright, but even more interesting because a big part of what makes you who you are is visible for all the world to see! And the world wants to know you and how you came to be who you are!

Daughter, you are young and hip! So many wonderful things await you in this life; you don't have time for unhealthiness to prevent you from living your best life. The world is your platform, so gather up who you are in Jesus and be the mighty healthy vessel He created you to be so you rule with a purpose and without interruption. It's not in your nature to be sad or sick. You are of the bloodline of Jesus Christ!

Remember as you get older, your physical organs will get older, too, and they become more vulnerable to imbalances that can lead to disease. Now, at your age, is a good time to begin to take care of your body so that when you're older, the chances of your body succumbing to disease are lessened.

Taking care of your body can be fun and exciting! You should begin with a plan that involves regular exercise, making healthy food choices, and annual visits to your family doctor.

Have fun doing research on the types of food that heal and nourish the body. Ask your family to try these new foods with you as you commit to adding healthy foods you've never tried before to your diet. Look at the foods in your home's pantry and begin to read the ingredient lists.

To nourish your mind, begin to value your quiet time to meditate and pray. When you feel bad or toxic thoughts come into your mind, redirect those by replacing them with thoughts and ideas that make you smile. If you feel you need help to redirect your mind, talk to your parents, and they can perhaps help or get the help you need.

Like everything else about you, the health of your body and mind is important to God, so it should be important to you. Imagine trying to take a test at school or perform a task at work while you're tired or in pain or distracted by unhealthy thoughts. Sometimes your work can be compromised when you're not feeling well.

Paul tells the Corinthians our bodies are the temple of God, and when we don't take care of it, we are bringing dishonor to Him. The state of your heart and spirituality is most important to God, but He wants you to take care of the physical body and your mind too.

Social well-being is of dire importance too. The way you connect and interact with other people in society will always be an opportunity for you to grow, to stretch yourself beyond what you may feel your personal character limitations are. God created humans to socialize. The alternative is self-isolation. Our personal socialization begins early when we are babies and can flourish from there because from the point of birth we are always interacting with the outside world: at school, jobs, clubs and organizations, in the grocery store, at sporting events. We are always interacting socially. How well we learn to socialize depends largely on learning to do so. Learning to socialize effectively can happen when you challenge yourself to interact in social settings.

## Wearing Emeralds

Make a list of things you can do to begin to take better care of your body. Remember to also list things that originate in our emotions and travel to our minds since we've already determined the body, mind, and spirit are related to good health.

_____

_____

_____

_____

_____

_____

_____

_____

_____

_____

_____

_____

_____

_____

_____

_____

_____

_____

## Word Power

Resilient: *Able to withstand or recover quickly from difficult conditions.*

Describe a difficult situation you encountered and write about how you recovered.

_____

_____

_____

_____

_____

_____

_____

_____

_____

_____

_____

_____

_____

_____

_____

_____

_____

_____

Nicole Stephens
For Mariella and Sisely

*"Soak in solitude. Savor the moment to enrich
your soul and find your joy."*

## CHAPTER 10

# Your Solitude

*Foremost*

What do you think solitude is? Solitude is being alone with yourself to capture the freeness of your thoughts and bring life to what those thoughts have the potential to birth. Solitude is all about you and you being present in the moment you've designated for you to renew your mind.

Now, that's my own personal definition of solitude because I practice solitude, and that's what my experience has produced. But *Webster's Dictionary*, however, defines solitude as the state of being alone and apart from others. That's it! I like my definition better. Maybe Mr. or Mrs. Webster has never practiced solitude and so cannot fully feel the definition of solitude. (Where do dictionary words get their meanings from anyway? Like who makes the definitions? Maybe I can help out in that department.)

When you begin to practice solitude, perhaps you, too, will define what it means for you. That is my hope. Solitude is so important, and hopefully by the end of this chapter, you will understand why. Solitude will change your life when practiced regularly.

In my solitude I dream—some days big, some days small, but I dream. I sit by a certain window in our house and allow the beautiful view to take me to places sometimes I feel impossible to get to unless I am in my solitude, dreaming. My view has a landscape lined with perfectly manicured trees, with skies so blue that it confirms that only the hand of God could create it. I dream of doing things I've always wanted to do, and I see clearly how to get there.

Sometimes in my solitude I write poetry or stories and books. It's easy for me to become the character I'm writing about, the one I try to define and then give life to, in my solitude. My creativity takes life, and I am birthing something that I hope will cause someone's perspective to be transformed.

Sometimes I pray or worship in my solitude. I hear a song that sentiments the exact feeling I have, and I lift my hands to the Holy One, belting the words in honor of Him. Other times I imagine—imagine what heaven is like or what my daughters will be like as young women living on their own. Sometimes in my solitude I watch the family of birds that built a nest in one of the trees, and I marvel at what great care the mother takes of the little ones. They wait with their beaks open, and she swoops in dropping the evening's meal in their beaks. I remember the first time I watched it. It was beautiful to watch, and I teared thinking, *How can anyone think there is no God!* That's what happens in my solitude.

I can't quite remember how I came to value solitude, but I know I did quite young. It was the time somewhere between elementary school and middle school. But I have vivid memories of what it was like and what I did. You can do these same things to find solitude.

1. Find the quietest, calmest place in your home or perhaps your backyard. Allow the only stimuli to be visual. Like things in nature—the sky, trees, birds—no sound.
2. If you can without falling asleep, close your eyes.
3. Focus on yourself and what it feels like to be alone with yourself.
4. Plan your designated times for your solitude.

I also know that when I was younger practicing solitude, the hopes and dreams I had I am living today. I dreamed about being a writer, a published author. I hoped to be a communicator. God breathed life on my hopes and dreams as I sat quiet and alone with myself and with him, positioning myself for the breath of life.

What do you do in your solitude? That time you take to escape mentally and physically, to be alone with yourself, to be alone with God. What do you do? What do you do when your mind is so bombarded with lists of things to do, the day's mishaps, and tomorrow's fears?

Being alone with yourself allows you to capture those times of calm that we often yearn for amidst the busy lives we lead. Your solitude centers you, renews your spirit, and allows you to clearly plan to do what you do more effectively. Solitude can prepare you for a difficult circumstance, a big decision, or just a moment to dream of your future.

Throughout the Bible there are examples of Jesus Christ Himself practicing solitude! So, if the Son of the one true God needed solitude, then certainly you and I do. Luke 22:39–46 describes the most pivotal time in Jesus' earthly journey before He would be crucified. He stole away to the Garden of Gethsemane for solitude. At this time in His solitude, He prayed!

> And He withdrew from them [disciples] about a stone's throw, and He knelt down and began to pray saying, "Father if You are willing, remove this cup from Me; yet not my will, but yours be done." ...And being in agony He was praying very fervently; and His sweat became like drops of blood, falling down upon the ground.
>
> Luke 22:41–44 (NASB)

Seeking solitude means withdrawing from the normal practices of the day's moments, withdrawing from people, places, and things that often symbolize distractions in our lives to do whatever it is that will bring you to a place of calm and centeredness. That place that will recharge you so that you can begin again.

Girl, the Bible also gives numerous accounts of many people getting alone with themselves and God. Elijah went to Mount Carmel for solitude to pray for rain when the country was in a drought. Solitude is such a time of mental, physical, and spiritual renewal. It's a sweet time to be alone with yourself and with God. Begin to practice solitude if you don't already, and see in the quiet of the moments yourself in your future succeeding in all areas of your life. Hear in the quiet of the moments what

God will say to you and be in the quiet of the moment still—breathing in His presence as you dream or pray or worship or draw near or hope or imagine, but just be still!

A dear friend of mine, now the mother of six, once told me the story of a moment in her solitude that nearly took my breath away. She and her husband had spent most of the day celebrating their son's third birthday along with family and friends. There were more than fifty kids and their parents at the party my friend and her husband threw to celebrate their son. My friend said she was exhausted by the end of the night and stole away to her closet to be alone. Shortly thereafter, she heard her three-year-old son knocking at the door of the closet. When she let him in, he found her sitting on the floor. She said she looked at him in wonder and awe, gazing at his beauty, but words for the moment didn't come. He, however, mistook her countenance for sadness as he knelt in front of her. He then put his hands, one on each side of her cheeks, and looked into her eyes and said, "Mommy, thank you for my birthday." She began to weep bitterly as the harsh memories of her pregnancy rushed to her mind. You see, when my friend was pregnant, it was such a difficult and stressful pregnancy. She was very sick, and her quality of life declined rapidly. So much so that she thought about terminating the pregnancy. I remember her calling me the day she was anticipating abortion. It was very sad and filled with emotion as we cried together with the heaviness weighing both our hearts. I remember praying with her and encouraging her to persevere because one day she would celebrate the fact that she endured the pregnancy. Hearing her son, now three years old, thank her for his "birthday," not his birthday party, she felt peace, joy, and calm finally fill her spirit. The years of guilt she felt dissipated in a moment when God gave her son the exact words to say at the perfect time she needed. That was in her solitude.

To be alone with yourself and with God begins a process of thinking more clearly, planning more strategically, and a renewing of your mind and spirit. When you are able to think clearly, you can plan extraordinarily. When you are able to plan extraordinarily, you open your mind to the possibility of embracing new things that will empower you to make an amazing difference in your life and in the lives of those of the world. You're a world changer. The world may seem big to you, but changing the world begins with changing your home, then your school, then your community, then your city, then your state, then your country. Changing the world means fighting where you are for change to take place there, and then before you know it, as you grow older, you will be where God destined you to be, and you will be working to change the world there as well.

Yes. All this can come from a repeated practice of embracing your solitude. What will you experience in your solitude? Will you hear the voice of God bring an answer you have been waiting for? Will you discover a passion for writing or drawing or singing? Will you finally forgive someone you've been needing to forgive? Will you look across a landscape to find trees swaying in the wind and the bluest sky as its backdrop, staying there for a moment as you discover God? Will you discover something about yourself? What will you experience...in your solitude?

## Wearing Emeralds

Create your own definition of *solitude* and what it means to you.

Write down the dates for three times you will steal away to be alone with yourself. Write your experience in the space below.

_____

_____

_____

_____

_____

_____

_____

_____

_____

_____

_____

_____

_____

_____

_____

_____

_____

_____

## Word Power

Foremost: *Most prominent in rank, importance, or position.*

Why do you think solitude should be one of the foremost things we practice as girls?

_____

_____

_____

_____

_____

_____

_____

_____

_____

_____

_____

_____

_____

_____

_____

_____

_____

_____

_____

Michelle Wheeler
For Mariah

*"Time is a gift. Treasure it. Make the most of now. Manage it wisely, and don't take it for granted. Don't put off until tomorrow what you can do, be, or give today."*

CHAPTER 11

# Your Time

*Valuable*

Dear Daughter, your time is valuable, plain and simple! That's it in a nutshell! Enough said!

Okay, let's rewind a little. People say all those phrases when they want to ascribe a serious nature and tone to what is preceded. But I don't think when we talk about time anything is ever really "plain and simple" or "in a nutshell." Nor is there "enough said" about how important it is to value our time. Professional life coaches and motivational speakers alike will tell you how important it is to design your goals around time management. Having good time management skills can be the difference between success and failure. Here are some simple examples of how success and failure are related to time and some outcomes of when maturation is not allowed or is interrupted.

1. The boiling of an egg. If an egg is not boiled for the amount of time needed to be fully cooked, salmonella poisoning can occur, causing sickness.
2. When a woman becomes pregnant, she is told by her doctor birth will occur at nine months. When birth occurs before then, sometimes health complications occur in both the mother and child.
3. If wine is opened too soon or too late, the aging process is interrupted and can negatively affect the taste and smell.

There are countless other examples of how time is related to success and failure. Showing you these examples is to reiterate how not respecting time can cause chaos. Can you think of times in the past when you were not successful in some way but now realize that if you had managed your time better, you would have a different outcome? I sure can. I think we all can. How does this make you feel—to know that you would have a completely different, more successful outcome if you had just timed things differently, if perhaps you had a plan to manage your time? And although that is time lost and you won't get that time back, you can move forward with a plan to manage your time. Here are some simple tips related to overcommitting your time.

1. Decide what you can and cannot commit to and set boundaries based on those parameters.
2. Decide what you will or will not commit to and set boundaries based on those parameters.

3. Practice these in your mind:
   I can and I will (only if I decide to)
   I can't, so I won't (I have decided)

Time is a valuable gift from God that we sometimes take for granted. First, the older you grow, the more you will find there are more constraints on your time, with school being the most pressing, followed by extracurricular activities, jobs, and spending time with family and friends. The lack of time management can cause you to become stressed and anxious as you feel pulled in many different directions. When you don't implement good time management practices, stress and anxiety can become a normal way of life for you without you even realizing it. Then, the high-paced, stressful lifestyle will lead to negative effects in your life, from missing the deadline on the school or work project to forgetting an appointment with a friend and maybe even sickness.

God wants your time to be structured for your own good, beginning each day with Him. I know, most days you begin rushing about your home to get dressed, eat breakfast, and head out the door. You may believe you don't have time to get alone with God. But I would like to challenge you to try getting up fifteen minutes sooner just to spend time talking to God about the details of your day. When you begin each day with a few minutes alone with God, it's an opportunity for you to talk to Him about your day and the expectations you have for succeeding in the things you have planned. Not only that, but you can ask God during this time to order your day as He ordains it to unfold—syncing your plan with His. Try it and you will begin to feel less stressed about your day because you'll grow to value the structure and order as you spend the first part of your day with God. You will begin to realize that when you give God control of your time, everything is in control because He is in control of everything. His timing for the circumstances of our lives is perfect.

"He has made everything appropriate in its time."

Ecclesiastes 3:11

This means everything has a season of birthing, of success according to God's purpose—so no matter how much you push, manipulate, and orchestrate, if it's not God's timing, it will not succeed. Whew! Don't you feel a load off already? Spend the first fruits of your time with Him to get His plan for your plans. Doing that will sound something like, "Hey, God, what do You think about this?" Once you get into the habit of consulting God about things that will require your time, you will find you will have extra time, less stress, and a growing relationship with the Father.

So how do you begin to give God your time? Each morning, just out of bed or still in bed as the case can be, write down everything you need to get accomplished in the day ahead. Or, if you like, list them all in your head. Then just tell God those are your plans for the day, and you are giving Him complete control of what happens and how it will happen. Thank Him for the gift of time. It's as simple as that.

Secondly, the effects of being idle can be devastating on our characters when we don't engage in productive things. For many years, beginning very young, my daughters were not allowed to watch television except on Fridays and Saturday mornings. My husband and I made that decision when they were very young so that they engaged in things that enriched their time as well as their minds. As a result of this being a standard rule in our home, I was careful, especially in summer, to ensure they were not idle. Honestly, it was such a wonderful time playing board games, reading great books, playing a sport, learning a foreign language, and learning musical instruments. They were having such a fantastic time during the week that when the weekend rolled around, they forgot they were allowed to watch television and continued all the other activities instead! To this day, at nineteen and twenty-three, my daughters are not big fans of watching television.

Interestingly, the apostle Paul warns us about being idle with our time and uses very colorful vocabulary to describe the widows that were. Speaking of widows in 1 Timothy 5:13, Paul says, "At the same time they also learn to be idle, as they go around from house to house; and not merely idle but also gossips and busy bodies talking about things not proper to mention." Ouch! Does that sound serious, or what? Have you ever found yourself speaking disparagingly about one friend to another friend? What prompts you to engage in idle gossip? Idle time! Daughter, make the most of your free time by engaging in things that will benefit you in the long run and will edify others and yourself. Your time is valuable! I know this verse was referenced just a few chapters prior, but it is apropos for this moment as well. Philippians 4:8 says, "Finally, brethren, whatever is true, whatever is honorable, whatever is right, whatever is pure, whatever is lovely, whatever is of good repute, if there is any excellence and if anything, worthy of praise, dwell on these things."

That's how you spend your time! When you spend time with other people, ensure those people are worthy of your time. Trust me, it's a really bad feeling when you realize you have wasted time with someone who was not worthy of your time because only destructive things came from the time. That's time you cannot get back, but you can move forward having learned from the experience of spending time with someone who's not worthy of you, doing things that could jeopardize the future God ordained you to have.

When my girls were younger, we played a game called "What Time Is It?" The point of the game was to remind them to do different things with their time and make wise choices in doing so. So I would at some points during the day ask, "Hey, Kerrigan or Kierstin, what time is it?" Kerrigan or Kierstin would respond, "It's time to read!" Or "It's time to play Legos!" Or "It's time to pick up my room!" It was a wonderfully enriching game that challenged them to be creative as well as teach them at a very young age the importance of using their time wisely. But superseding all that, I had given them a choice as to how they would like to structure the moment. Time.

Use your time to plan to be successful by being intentional on how you choose to spend your time. Teach this to your friends and their friends, and before you know it, you will be spending your time building things you can use to help you make a difference in your environment, in your world. One thing girls like you are purposed to do is build things that will benefit your environment. By "things" I mean programs born from a wonderful idea you have or relationships with like-minded, influential people you meet or perhaps a legacy of your gifts and talents. The time you use can never be retrieved, so why not use the time to do things that define your place in this world?

Girl, your time is valuable! Make the most of it by living intentionally and purposefully.

## Wearing Emeralds

Use the space below to list ways you can organize your time. Identify idleness in your time and list ways you can use time more wisely.

_____

_____

_____

_____

_____

_____

_____

_____

_____

_____

_____

_____

_____

_____

_____

_____

_____

_____

_____

_____

## Word Power

Valuable: *Something that is of great worth.*

Do you have anything you hold dear that is of value to you? Describe why it is.

_____

_____

_____

_____

_____

_____

_____

_____

_____

_____

_____

_____

_____

_____

_____

_____

_____

_____

_____

_____

*"Looking back will not help you to move forward into the future. Dwelling on the past slows you down. Learn from your mistakes, take the positive, and keep moving forward. This will help you reach your goals sooner."*

### CHAPTER 12

# Your Past

*Forgiven*

Dear Daughter, forgiveness is something that can have a considerable effect on our personal well-being. Considerable. Being able to forgive ourselves and others is paramount. The greatest book ever written speaks immeasurably about forgiveness. "Be kind to one another, tender-hearted, forgiving each other, just as God in Christ has forgiven you" (Ephesians 4:32). As I have grown both chronologically and spiritually, my relationship with forgiveness has evolved and changed as my relationship with myself and God has. I can more easily forgive people and myself now. But here's the thing. Let me save you some heartache on your journey to self-introspection and destiny. Because that's what this book is about. There is no gray area about forgiveness. You either do or don't. You either will or won't. You either can or can't. I wish someone had put it plain and simple for me the way I am about to put it for you! Keep reading.

First, let's look at the structure of forgiveness. It's been my experience that forgiveness has what I have labeled three arms or prongs. These are circumstances surrounding forgiveness that we have unknowingly created and unconsciously practice in our lives. Let me just preface this by saying they're all wrong!

1. *You easily forgive yourself but not others.* This can look like you are holding others accountable for their infractions but giving yourself a pass when you make mistakes and fall short. It feels good to you because, in your mind, you never do anything wrong, especially nothing requiring forgiveness.

2. *You easily forgive others but not yourself.* This can be because you hold yourself to a higher standard. Subconsciously you think you are better than the average person, and you believe you cannot afford to make the same mistakes others do.

3. *You don't forgive yourself very easily, nor do you forgive others easily.* This can be because you think nobody deserves forgiveness.

But *everyone* deserves forgiveness. God forgives *everyone.* Even the worst criminal. And yes, that seems unfair because the things people do to us are wrong. It seems our own wrongdoings against other people shouldn't carry the same weight of a murderer! But the weight of the cross on His back was the weight of the world on His back. It bore the same heaviness.

Sin bears the same heaviness although some sin has greater consequences than others.

When you ask God to forgive you for a wrongdoing, He immediately forgives you! *Immediately!* He's not like we are in our humanness. He doesn't ponder whether He will forgive you, nor does He forgive you based on how He may be feeling the day you ask. He doesn't recall the previous seventy times He had to forgive you. He forgives you in the very moment you ask for forgiveness, and it's forgotten—never to be brought to His remembrance ever again. Sometimes we wrongly ascribe human characteristics to God Almighty. You or your friends may take time to fully forgive because you are hurt and wounded by the wrong that has been done to you. It's wrong to hold a person's sin or mistake against them by continuously bringing it up over and over in your mind and to the person. We are charged with mirroring who God is, and God forgives immediately!

"If we confess our sins, He is faithful and righteous to forgive us our sins and to cleanse us from all unrighteousness" (1 John 1:9).

It's so important that you look back on your past mistakes and assess the circumstances surrounding the choice you made resulting in the mistake. For this reason, your past is invaluable! Do you realize that? You get to look back on your past life to help with your present and future. Think about it. Would you ever intentionally repeat an action that caused you to stumble and caused consequences to your life that were threatening to your future? What's more important is that you forgive yourself for those mistakes.

Everyone makes mistakes; everyone does. But here is a vital piece of information that will help you to make wiser choices.

Think back to that moment when you made the mistake you are too ashamed to talk about and that is painful to remember. Before you carried through the mistake, did you feel a sense that you shouldn't follow through with the action that caused you to stumble? Did your inner voice tell you not to do it? Did you feel anxious or nervous or scared? Were you consumed with a heaviness that made you uneasy? Girl, all those things describe your inner spirit rising up in you so greatly urging you to stop! It communed with the Holy Spirit, who was urging you not to move forward!

One of the many roles of the Holy Spirit in our lives is to give us strength and help in our fight against negative circumstances in our lives. Before Jesus ascended to heaven, He instructed His disciples, "You shall receive power when the Holy Spirit comes upon you and you shall be witnesses to Me in Jerusalem, and in all Judea and Samaria, and to the end of the earth" (Acts 1:8).

Sometimes we ignore that inner voice, that urging of the Holy Spirit, and it is then the mistake occurs. The Bible states in 1 Corinthians 10:13, "No temptation has overtaken you except such as is common to man; but God is faithful, who will not allow you to be tempted beyond what you are able, but with the temptation will also make the way of escape, that you may be able to bear it."

The key to your past being a tool you can use for success in your present life and future is not feeling shame, regret, or insecurity about things you've done or things that may have happened to you that are painful. Sometimes the pain runs deep, but the love of the Father is deeper than the deepest ocean, and

He says you are still beautiful, strong, wonderful, and brave! So very brave that nothing can separate you from all He has destined for you. So it is time to move from your past and live fully in your present. Use your past to empower you, not to destroy you.

When you allow yourself or other people to cause you to feel shame about your past, you have given away the power God gave you. Think about it—playing the things that cause us shame over and over in our minds prevents us from moving forward in new thoughts and ideas that God plants there for us to grow. Your infractions may be great in your eyes, but His love is greater than anything you will ever experience. Daughter, our God is an amazing God! He loves you so much. He does not want you to jeopardize your present and future by continuing to live in the past. Oh, taste and see that the Lord is good and His mercy endures forever!

Of course, your past can hold the fondest of memories as well—wonderful, heartwarming memories you want to hold on to forever. So do. Keep those dear to your heart. Perhaps write them down so you don't forget.

The day my family and I moved from our very first house to the house we currently live in was a bittersweet moment for us all. We were sad because we began to recall all the sweet memories of the house we were leaving held. It was our very first house, so we experienced a lot of firsts there. My girls came home from the hospital to the most beautiful nursery on the days they were born. I homeschooled them there, and I remember at lunchtime we fished in the lake behind our backyard but always threw the fish back into the pond because the girls "didn't want them to be without their families." I laughed inside each time I heard them say that. My girls were blessed with two big brothers when their cousins came to live with us for two years. It was the most fun we had ever had in that house: the Christmases and birthdays, the backyard barbecues, the walks along the water outlining our backyard, the out-of-town guests who found solace there. Those fond memories can paint our hearts with joy that falls upon us like a warm, cozy blanket of comfort when it's cold, cold outside.

Your past is designed to help you grow in things that will benefit your present and your future. It should shape your de-cision-making process in large part to live a present and future that is not predisposed to innumerable mistakes. I cannot say this enough. You are going to make mistakes. We all will. It's a natural progression of life. But use your past to your advantage by visiting it from time to time to extract from it what you need to shape your present and future. Not to beat yourself up about things that you've done that shame you. The key to being able to do that effectively is not getting stuck there.

When the memories are not fond ones and you are still liv-ing there, in the past, you are probably reliving pain and hurt. Remember God wants to see you live in the present so that you are preparing for the future He has planned for you. He wants to give you the future He created for you so that you have a new opportunity to begin again on the other side of your past. What's most important about not allowing your past mistakes to overwhelm your mind and heart is to believe God when He says you are forgiven, and He loves you no matter what you've done, no matter where you've been, and no matter what your bumps, bruises, and wounds are. Run to the Father for healing of your past because He is the only One that can assure you that you can begin to live life to the fullest, leaving behind the hurts of your past, embracing the present possibility, and trusting Him for things of your future.

## Wearing Emeralds

List the things in your past you want to forgive yourself for. What do you need to forgive someone else for? How do you think your past can prevent you from growing?

_____

_____

_____

_____

_____

_____

_____

_____

_____

_____

_____

_____

_____

_____

_____

_____

_____

_____

_____

_____

## Word Power

Forgiven: *To have a debt canceled.*

How do you know when you have truly forgiven someone?

_____

_____

_____

_____

_____

_____

_____

_____

_____

_____

_____

_____

_____

_____

_____

_____

_____

_____

_____

Shannon Sims
For Carley

*"When you are focused and embracing your courageous spirit, those around you are inspired to do the same, making fear tremble in His presence."*

## CHAPTER 13

# Your Present

*Emergent*

Dear Daughter, one of my all-time favorite movies is *Dead Poets Society*. It is set in 1959, and Robin Williams is Professor John Keating at the fictitious Vermont elite and conservative boys boarding school, Welton Academy. His approach to teaching, ideology, and methodology are rejected, criticized, and ridiculed by faculty members and the administration but enthusiastically embraced and emulated by his students. Professor Keating's thematic message is carpe diem. Carpe diem, at first mention, seems bewildering because of its Latin origin, but the meaning of this term is wealthy with thematic promise: seize the day!

I've probably seen *Dead Poets Society* about five or six times, not counting the times I'm channel surfing and it's unexpectedly airing. Each time I watch it, even in small segments, I get something more than the previous times I watched. But the foundational message is the same: make the most of each day, be present in the present, bring what you are supposed to bring to the world as soon as you know, and don't waste your time.

You are young and beautiful with the potential to be anyone you want to be and to do anything you desire! In order to live an enriching and successful life ordained by God, you must seize the day. Smart girls plan for their futures by seizing the present moment.

Professor Keating shaped the young minds of his students encouraging them to take seriously the journey they were on, relaying to them that whatever they do in the present, deposits into their futures. He taught them how to consciously choose how to spend each waking moment of their days.

Making the most of the present moment will require you to manage time well, take full advantage of opportunities set before you, and create your own opportunities that will lead to the future you were destined to live. When you choose to make the most of each day, you are actually doing things that will prepare you for a successful future. Do you know you are created to do great things in life? Yes! You. Despite what you may feel or what someone may have told you, it's true that you are created to do great and amazing things in life; the world needs your input. You are destined for greatness. You were created to become a change-maker of the world. Your strength is unsurpassed. Your ideas are creative. Your voice is needed. But your destiny begins with self-introspection coupled with seizing the moment you are currently in and setting goals that will enable you to arrive at your destiny.

The goals you set will require a steadfast, unmovable approach to accomplish them. Here's how to start: learning the power of procrastination and distractions.

1. Recognize that procrastination is designed to prevent you from accomplishing things that shape a successful future. A girl ready to walk confidently into her future recognizes procrastination is not her friend. In fact, it is her enemy. Procrastination is delaying a task that needs to be accomplished. When you continuously and repeatedly defer initiating completion of a task, you risk settling into a life where there is no progress toward accomplishing your goals. Where does that leave the world? Short of one less warrior girl! When procrastination becomes a habit, you begin to live the life of a mundane, ordinary girl.

2. Recognize what distractions are. All distractions aren't bad. They don't all look the same, but they are all designed to prevent you from accomplishing a task. A lunch invitation from a friend you haven't seen in a while is wonderful. Unless the time designated for the lunch date is time you should be fulfilling a task you've procrastinated doing.

A good practice that has worked wonderfully for me is to put my tasks and goals on a schedule with beginning and end dates. I allot portions of each day for a certain amount of the task to be completed in a given day. I complete at least what's scheduled for that day. No less, but sometimes more. It's tough sticking to a schedule, but the feeling I get after a task has been completed is one of accomplishment.

Seize each day by putting God first each day. It is not going to be easy putting God first and not thinking and worrying about the responsibilities of each day. By spending time alone with God first, He will ensure you meet every task of the day and satisfy each responsibility. But, Daughter, the more you practice putting God first each day and focusing on the tasks of your life, it will become a wonderful habit that will reap rewards to your relationship with Him, with yourself, and with others. Always be aware of living your fullest life today, and God will take great care of your future!

> "Therefore be careful how you walk, not as unwise men but as wise, making the most of your time, because the days are evil."
>
> Ephesians 5:15–16

We are to make the most of every chance we get, not living carelessly and aimlessly allowing the influences of the world to capture our hearts. Yes, you are to take responsibility for the accomplishments of your day, the course of your day, but God does not want you to worry about anything! He says that if you put Him first in every area of your life, He will take care of everything that concerns you. So seizing the opportunities of each day does not mean worrying about your future or the present life you live.

I learned a valuable lesson in planning and not worrying several years ago. In August 2005, Hurricane Katrina destroyed the city of New Orleans. The days and hours leading up to the moment Hurricane Katrina made landfall, thousands of New Orleanians were mandated to evacuate the city. It was one of the biggest evacuations in New Orleans history. Many people were ordered to leave their homes for cities that were nearby. However, my immediate family members—Mother, Father, siblings, and their families—came to live with our family in Texas. As we waited through the night for twenty-three people to arrive, we knew we would embrace them with open hearts and open arms, but anxiety began to set into our minds. We worried about how long we would be able to afford the massive grocery bills and all the bills that came with running a home. The uncertainty of how long they would need to live with us played over and over in our minds. We were afraid of what the days ahead would bring. After talking about it, my husband and I began to disregard the anxiety attached to whelming thoughts. We knew that God's sovereignty was bigger than any fear, any bills, and any anxiety. We knew that He wanted us to help our family members and anyone else who needed help, so He would provide the resources we needed to help those in need. We knew that the savings my husband had built for us were enough to help our extended family if it was needed.

Once in our home, we began to enjoy them being there, sharing meals with us, watching television shows, and playing board games. It was such a fun-filled time we sometimes forgot the underlying reason why they were there.

On the third day of them all having stayed at our home, I left to pick up Kierstin, then a kindergartener at Pierce Private Day School. When I drove into the carpool lane, every teacher, administrator, student, and parent affiliated with the school stood in the driveway with signs that read, "God bless you," "We love you," and "God is amazing!" As I parked and disembarked my car, walking toward the crowd, I wondered what was being celebrated and why I hadn't received correspondence informing me of this wonderful parade and in whose honor we were celebrating. Once I approached closer to the crowd, they all began hugging me and telling me how wonderful I was. I immediately thought, *Oh no! I hope Kierstin did not tell them it was my birthday*. My birthday was nine months off. My heart sank. But when they ushered me through the doors of the school, the lobby of this sweet, little school was filled with blankets, water bottles, toiletries, and enough food to feed a small army! And standing in the middle of it all was Kierstin, smiling the biggest smile I had ever seen light her face. My beautiful girl had told her teacher, who told her principal, who told her owner of the school, who told all the parents affiliated with the school, who told God, that Kierstin's extended family had come to live with us as a result of fleeing New Orleans from Hurricane Katrina! They all banded together and collected so many things, it was perfect enough to feed, clothe, and comfort all twenty-three family members for the two months they lived in our home.

So, while we are worrying about the details of our lives, God is crafting those details to be exactly what we need in the moment we need them. Our God is an amazing God and will do things that will send our minds into a whirlwind and our hearts into calm. As a result, Daughter, don't worry about provision for your future as you live here in the present. It is the most beneficial to us to take every chance to seize opportunities of each day. As you are living in the present moment with your plan on how you will contribute to blessing the world in hand, put God first, seize the day, and go confidently into your future!

## Wearing Emeralds

Think about all the things you worry about. How do you feel as you are worrying? Now memorize Matthew 6:31–33. Use the space below to write the ways you will begin to "seize the day."

_____

_____

_____

_____

_____

_____

_____

_____

_____

_____

_____

_____

_____

_____

_____

_____

_____

_____

_____

_____

## Word Power

Emergent: *In the process of coming into being or becoming prominent.*

Examine a typical day in your life. Are you recognizing opportunities that you could use to prepare for your future? What things will you do to begin to take advantage of your present time in planning for your future?

_____

_____

_____

_____

_____

_____

_____

_____

_____

_____

_____

_____

_____

_____

_____

_____

_____

_____

Melody Jackson
For Khaelyn

*"Life should be soul-fulfilling, continuously evolving, open-mind-thrilling, word-problem-solving, a-lot-of-love-spilling, people-involving, God-instilling until the world stops spinning."*

## CHAPTER 14

# Your Future

*Brilliant*

Dear Daughter, first things first. Your future is filled with such promise and possibility! You should be very excited about your future now that you are actively seeking to learn about your identity and destiny. And now that you are willing to make the necessary changes to set you on the path to learning who you are and who you can become, you have changed the trajectory and course of your future and your life. It's evidenced by you picking up and reading this book and others like it. The moment you did, God was thrilled for you—thrilled that you now know that you can have everything He has for you—and it was all good. Do you know you are destined for greatness? Yes, greatness! But what is destiny, and what is greatness? Why are you given a destiny, and how do you know it will be great? These are all questions you're probably asking yourself.

Destiny, as defined by the Bible, is being preordained by God to use the gifts and talents He created you with to do good works in the earth so that He is glorified in you—that's destiny in a nutshell! You were given a destiny by God to serve others so that others would see the greatness by which you live your life and would come to know Jesus as a result. God will be glorified.

> "We are his workmanship, created in Christ Jesus for good works, which God prepared beforehand, that we should walk in them."
>
> Ephesians 2:10

Can you imagine what the world would look like if each and every one of us knew exactly what we were gifted and talented to do and used those gifts to live in purpose and our destiny? It would indeed be a better place.

While no one can predict the future—only God can—we can all prepare ourselves for the future. Does that sound contradictory to you? It did to me when I was your age. How do you prepare yourself for the unknown?

Well, you're not actually preparing yourself for the unknown. You're actually planning and mapping out a route to use what you know to be your gifts. It doesn't matter that we don't know the future. God knows it. We can't know what He knows about the future. What you can know today is that no matter what the world is like in the future, if you begin to embrace the idea that you have a destiny and it begins with knowing who you are, it won't matter what the world looks like. You will be living in purpose, and you'll be positioned to rule in your area of expertise.

I think if it becomes commonplace for girls to think of the future as that time and place when their destiny has been revealed and they become excited about living out their destiny, they will be more apt to begin the journey. So here are some ways to prepare for destiny, for your future, for the journey:

1. Identify your passion. Our passions lead us to knowledge of what our gifts and talents are.
2. Nurture your gifts and talents. If you do not practice and use your gifts, you will lose your gifts.
3. Partner (or hang out with) people who share your passion. There is nothing like a community of other people who love what we love.
4. Assess whether or not you can be compensated when offering your passion as a service. There will always come a point in your life when you will be compensated financially for what you are passionate about. Think about when that should be for you. It could be now. What are you waiting for? Your gift is worth financial compensation.

Daughter, when you begin the journey to reaching your destiny, using the concepts above to get started, do not worry about the unknown. Remember you're not supposed to know the unknown because there is nothing unknown to God and He is guiding you if you ask for His direction. Remember He created you, so He knows everything about you: what your gifts and talents are, what your destiny is, and what your journey will be like on the road to your destiny. He knows the roadblocks put in your way. He's already gone ahead and removed them. He knows the walls your enemies built to prevent you from walking through the door on the other side. He will teach you how to climb it. He sees the tree that has strategically been placed across the road you are supposed to walk. But He created that same tree and will command it to move and become planted in the soil again. Remember all of creation knows His name and bows at the mention of it! These aren't platitudes to be disregarded like cliches. They're facts. He said it.

You never need to worry about your future if you are seeking your destiny. Never! The Bible says, "'For I know the plans I have for you,' declares the LORD, 'plans for welfare and not for evil, to give you a future and a hope'" (Jeremiah 29:11). So even in the midst of trouble, God still has a plan for you. Before you were even born, God was thinking of you and deciding what He wanted your future to look like. Think about that. *Before* you were created physically, you were a thought of His, and He decided He wanted to use you to bring great things into this world in His name. What love is that? He chose you! He destined you for greatness.

I like challenges. Accomplishing them gives me such a sense of victory. I'd like to challenge you to think about what your destiny is and how it relates to what God wants you to do with your life. Imagine getting to the end of life as an older adult and never having realized or lived the destiny God has for you. By then it's too late. It's like receiving a beautifully wrapped present, placing it on a shelf, and never ever knowing what's inside because you didn't care to open it. Even more disheartening than that is the present inside the box is an amazing item God spent time handcrafting only for you, and nobody else can use it but you. Then one day you are at the end of your life, and you are reminded that the box is there still on the shelf. You reach for it, and it's comfortable in your hands. Inside you find a letter from God explaining what you are to do with the map, which is also inside the box. He says the map will take you on your life's journey and lead you to the treasure He created just for you. It showed you the roads to avoid and the ones that were safe to travel on. The map showed when the terrain would be rough and told you where to get the tools you needed to navigate the rough terrain. You gasp as the realization of the moment reveals that the box contained the gift from God of your destiny.

Girl! You do not want to get halfway through your life or at the end of it then decide to open the box to find the most amazing present from God. You want that present now! He wants to give it to you now! That present is your destiny. Ecclesiastes 12:1 says, "Remember also your Creator in the days of your youth, before the evil days come and the years draw near when you will say, I have no delight in them." That means while you are still young, God wants you to begin to seek Him for the plan for your life and wants to teach you how to use that plan as your part in helping to build the world and the kingdom.

I believe greatness is what you see in a person as a result of one using the gifts and talents given by God to develop and use in their day-to-day lives to help others. Of course, *Webster* says greatness is "the quality of being great, distinguished, eminent." I guess I can see that too.

Think about it. The more you do something, the better at it you become. When you decide to walk toward your destiny, it won't be easy every day. In fact, the enemy will line things up to prevent you from first making the decision to live out the plan God has for your life. Secondly, the enemy's plan is to prevent you from actually reaching your destiny. That's his job. He knows that if you, and other girls like you, work toward reaching the destiny God designed for you, he will be destroyed. Remember he wants to dismantle, destroy, and desecrate anything that will build the kingdom of God. As Christians, we are equipped to build the kingdom of God by sharing who God is with others in the hope they will join us in working to build the kingdom. God says, "I have given you authority to tread upon serpents and scorpions and over all the power of the enemy and nothing shall injure you" (Luke 10:19, NASB). So that's wonderful news! No matter what, no matter how, and no matter when the enemy attacks, you can declare your victory over him and what he is using to attack you. Remember when Jesus died on the cross? His death was to give us victory over the enemy. Colossians 2:15 says, "In this way, He disarmed the spiritual rulers and authorities. He shamed them publicly by His victory over them on the cross." So it doesn't matter what you are facing along the path to your destiny; you can be assured you will have the victory. And God will shame publicly those coming against you! Isn't that wonderful? Because you are a child of the one true God, you always have victory over the enemy. The difficult test you have in school, the job you were fired from, the broken friendship, the grandparents you miss, the soccer game you can't play in—it doesn't matter the problem, you always have the victory. Always! Step on him, kick him, or slice him into pieces and throw him off of a bridge, but get him off of your pathway and start back on your journey to your destiny—your journey to greatness. That's what's in your future!

## Wearing Emeralds

Remember the box I mentioned above? The one you were to imagine was given to you by God, with the most spectacular gift for your journey to your destiny. If you were given a box with a gift and your destiny was inside, what do you think would be inside? Use the space below to explain what you think would be inside and why.

_____

_____

_____

_____

_____

_____

_____

_____

_____

_____

_____

_____

_____

_____

_____

_____

_____

_____

## Word Power

Brilliant: *Very bright and radiant; exceptionally clever or talented.*

What about yourself would you describe as brilliant?

_____

_____

_____

_____

_____

_____

_____

_____

_____

_____

_____

_____

_____

_____

_____

_____

_____

_____

_____

_____

Darcy Bixby
For Courtney and Cami

*"You can spend your entire life running in circles and planning for 'what ifs' to avoid any chance of hurt and pain. Or you can stop running and hide under the magnificent shadow of His wings and surrender. To His Plan, what is."*

CHAPTER 15

# Your Victory

*Victorious*

Dear Christian Daughter, your victory is guaranteed. It's true. No matter what you are facing, no matter how big you think the problem is, your victory is guaranteed. You are going to win! Jesus' victory on the cross sealed your victory on earth in *any* circumstance you face in life! *Any* encompasses *all*. It doesn't matter how magnified the problem is to you. Nothing is too big for the Father. When you begin to understand this and live this, you will become fearless and confident to do things without the limits society can sometimes teach you. The key to victory over the circumstances you face is to acknowledge and embrace a relationship with the Father.

"For this is the love of God, that we keep His command-ments. And His commandments are not burdensome. For whatever is born of God overcomes the world. And this is the victory that has overcome the world—our faith."

1 John 5:3–4

Do you know what that means? If you believe that Jesus is the Son of God, that makes you a child of God. And if you are a child of God, you inherit the conquering power over anything anyone brings your way. It doesn't matter what it is. You will always have victory. It doesn't matter how big the problem; you will always have victory. I know I've probably said that somewhere else in this book, but I tend to repeat what is important to know.

Deuteronomy 20:1–4 says:

> When you go out to battle against your enemies and see horses, chariots, and people more numerous than you, do not be afraid of them; for the LORD your God, who brought you up from the land of Egypt, is with you. When you are approaching the battle, the priest shall come forward and speak to the people. He shall say to them, "Hear, Israel, you are approaching the battle against your enemies today. Do not be fainthearted. Do not be afraid, or panic, or be terrified by them, for the LORD your God is the One who is going with you, to fight for you against your enemies, to save you."

In the scripture above, the reference to "horses and chariots" indicates a clear advantage over the opponent. The chariot gave an unyielding speed by which the army would travel against their enemy, and the elevation of the chariot gave the occupant a clear advantage of height over his opponent. Also, historians believe the owners of "horses and chariots" were wealthy and advantaged. These are all things that can cause the seemingly disadvantaged to feel defeated before the battle even begins. Much like the battles we face today. But none of that matters when you are a child of the one true God. He goes before you and fights for you. He never loses.

Here, the priest was speaking to the Israelites about the war they were about to engage in. He was encouraging them to not be afraid because the size of their army paled in comparison to the size of the opposing army. This high priest's role was to ensure the men going to war were prepared physically and spiritually for the battle. When you are facing a battle or a problem that overwhelms you, you will need someone to encourage you, pray for you, direct you, someone to prepare you for the fight that lies ahead. You cannot go it alone. God never intends for us to fight our battles alone.

When you go to battle, you need a "priest," a friend, who will encourage and motivate you using the voice of God, the same way the priest in the scripture above encouraged and motivated the Israelis who were going to battle. He told them not to be afraid because God was with them, and they would have the victory. His words were comforting and motivating at the same time. His words gave them peace as they were going to war. Imagine feeling peaceful about a problem you are facing. Peace! That only happens when we know God is really the One fighting for us. Who in your life will be the "priest" before you head to the battle?

Some time ago I was facing one of the most difficult problems I had ever faced. I was hopeless and sad and felt devastated by the size of the problem that had consumed my life and heart so much that I cried often. As I poured out my heart to God, He sent me a dear friend whom I was able to share my hurt with. One day she said to me, "Khris, it feels like you're losing, but you're actually winning." I could not understand a word of what she'd said because it did feel like I was losing. So how could I actually be winning if everything about the situation looked like I was losing, and I felt strongly that I was losing? How? Because as long as you are being obedient to God, He is indeed working your problem out for your good. Romans 8:28 tells us, "And we know that ALL things God works for the good of those who love Him, and who have been called according to His purpose." So, although you may feel defeated, God is working behind the scenes and behind your feelings and crafting your victory. He is the master crafter!

Now, don't be surprised if your victory looks nothing like you were hoping it would look like or what you thought it should look like. Remember God is in control, and He is crafting your victory to be the best thing for you, not what you think is the best thing for you. It will be hard to let go of the feelings generated by this problem, but in order for the Father to fight for you, you must. If you begin to trust in God's ability to win this battle for you, you will see your victory sooner rather than later, and you will gain more after the battle is over than when you first entered into the battle. How amazing is our Father!

One of the most compelling and powerful examples of the influence and weightiness of God's intervening presence to cause astounding and staggering victory is the story of King Jehosophat's kingdom under attack. I kid you not. If you can understand the Bible's elucidation of this story, you will never question whether you will have victory again. (I'm crying as I write this because I found King Jehosophat's kingdom under attack at a very hard time in my life. My kingdom was under attack too!)

Second Chronicles 20 is where the story begins. Read it with anticipation and expectation. It will change your life. When Jehoshaphat's kingdom was under attack by three different armies—not one, not two, but three armies: Moabites, Ammonites, and Meunites—he was afraid for his people. Sometimes people will join forces against you. But that's okay. *When there is an alliance formed against you, it does not negate your win. It simply means that God is exposing several of your enemies to you at once.*

You will initially be afraid when you are facing something seemingly insurmountable. Jehoshaphat was afraid. Imagine the person leading you is shivering in fear. That's like when you see your parents afraid. Oh boy! You should be scared then, right? So here you have Jehoshaphat afraid because three armies were coming to war against his kingdom. He immediately prays. Then he announces the imminent attack to the people of his kingdom and instructs them to join him in a kingdom-wide time of fasting and praying.

His prayer:

> Lord, God of our fathers, are You not God in the heavens? And are You not ruler over all the kingdoms of the nations? Power and might are in Your hand so that no

one can stand against You. Did You not, our God, drive out the inhabitants of this land from Your people Israel, and give it to the descendants of Your friend Abraham forever? They have lived in it, and have built You a sanctuary in it for Your name, saying, "If disaster comes upon us, the sword, or judgment, or plague, or famine, we will stand before this house and before You (for Your name is in this house), and cry out to You in our distress, and You will hear and save us."

2 Chronicles 20:6–9

What Jehosaphat was saying here was, "Aren't You God? Don't You have all power? Don't You rule over evil? Isn't it true no one defeats You? Didn't You tell us to cry out to You in trouble, and You not only hear us, but You will help us?"

While assembled fasting and praying, God sent encouraging words by way of the prophet Jahaziel. He stood and said, "Listen all Judah and the inhabitants of Jerusalem and King Jehoshaphat: thus, says the Lord to you, 'Do not fear or be dismayed for the battle is not yours but God's. ...You need not fight in this battle. Station yourselves, stand, and see the salvation of the Lord'" (2 Chronicles 20:15–17). The next day when Jehoshaphat's army went out to the battleground, they found dead bodies. The three armies who had come to defeat Jehosaphat's army had turned on one another because God had set up ambushes! The three opposing armies left behind so many valuables: valuable garments, livestock, equipment, and many other valuable goods. It took Jehoshaphat's army three days to collect all the plunder to take back to their own kingdom.

So, you see, God will not only defeat your enemies for you, but you will come out of the battle with more than you entered into it with. This could mean more wisdom, knowledge, friends, a better grade on the next test, a need, and riches! When you are entrenched in battle, and you are seeking victory in Christ:

1.  Find your priest. The friend who will guide you and instruct you in the ways of God. This friend will be the one praying for and with you. You will recognize this friend because of their reputation for having a relationship with God.
2.  Don't look at the size and grandeur of your enemy's "things." God's "things" are bigger and grander.
3.  Show your faith and commitment to allowing God to fight your battle by fasting something for a period of time to focus on your deliverance and victory. This could be TV, social media, phone calls, etc.
4.  Expect to not only be victorious but to gain more after the battle than what you had before the battle started.

Girl, what battle are you facing? Who are you fighting against on your own? You may feel small and at a disadvantage because your opponent is bigger than you are. They have more things than you do. You feel you don't have everything you need to win this battle. You have no "horses and chariots," and the enemy is coming against you quickly! "So shall they fear the name of the Lord from the west, and his glory from the rising of the sun. When the enemy shall come in like a flood, the Spirit of the Lord shall lift up a standard against him" (Isaiah 59:19, KJV). Your victory is already determined. It's guaranteed.

## Wearing Emeralds

In the space provided below, list the battle you are facing.

Also, think over your friendships and acquaintances and list the friend, acquaintance, or parent who can be your "priest."

_____

_____

_____

_____

_____

_____

_____

_____

_____

_____

_____

_____

_____

_____

_____

_____

_____

_____

_____

_____

_____

_____

## Word Power

Victorious: *Having won, triumphant.*

Can you remember all the victories you've already experienced? Write them here, and as you do, remember victories can be big or small.

_____

_____

_____

_____

_____

_____

_____

_____

_____

_____

_____

_____

_____

_____

_____

_____

_____

_____

Mandy Jones
For Joylyn and Jayla

*"What you say carries the depth of a moment. Be careful of what you speak because your speech holds the power for amazing moments or moments that create despair. When moments are amazing, God is there."*

## CHAPTER 16

# Your Speech

*Eloquent*

Dear Daughter, what you speak is a part of who you are. Why is that true? When we speak, we are communicating what has been seeded in our core, in our spirits. We have watered it there and nurtured those things in our spirits, whether good or bad. Those seeds we water and nurture become how we think, feel, and ultimately how we act and what we speak. As a result, others around us know, simply by how we speak, the essence and core of who we really are. Our identity.

As a daughter of God, you are royalty and an heir to a mighty kingdom ruled by Him, the one true God. Being an heir to a throne so magnificent as God's is a huge responsibility, and much is expected of you. Aside from the expectations, your speech is to mirror God's as you are speaking. When God speaks, His words edify, encourage, compliment, discipline, praise, teach, and build relationships. His words encourage us to boldly live His truth in a world that designs our demise and works to silence our voices.

So how do we feed the core of who we are, our spirits, seeds that are positive so that what we communicate communicates that we are exceptional girls empowered to elevate our spheres?

1. Be conscious of what you say. Don't speak carelessly and unbridled. Plan to always speak to edify others and situations.
2. Don't allow others to cause you to say things you will regret. Control your emotions.
3. Commit to learning and being obedient to what the Bible says about blasphemy, evil speaking, whispering, and complaining and the effect these things have on relationships.

Girl, stand firm against blasphemy, evil speaking, whispering, and complaining. James 3:5–6 tells us:

> So...the tongue is a small part of the body, and yet it boasts great things. See how great a forest is set aflame by such a small fire! And the tongue is a fire, the very world of iniquity; the tongue is set among our members as that which defiles the entire body, and sets on fire the course of our life, and is set on fire by hell.

This means it only takes a spark, a small ember, to set off a forest fire. The same thing can happen if you speak the wrong word. You may think of something you've said as being small and insignificant, but it may, in fact, be something that can cause a barrage of damage. Remember the words you speak can ruin someone's reputation, bring discord to a situation, slander, and hurt someone emotionally.

Several years ago, I unintentionally hurt the feelings of a very dear friend who trusted me. We shared a friendship of respect, kindness of heart, and a sweet reliance on the other for familial support. Our families became like family to each other since each of our own immediate families were in different states and not always able to visit regularly.

On this particular Saturday evening, her family and mine were with mutual friends in a deep discussion about a topic of debate that was very dear to both of us, but we were on opposite sides of the issue. As a longtime debater of issues in high school and college, I was trained to cripple the other individual's stance quickly, which makes them insecure and unsure of continuing the debate, because typically they're not expecting an attack so soon. And certainly not one that could be interpreted as personal. Well, this was my friend of many years, and I wasn't debating an opponent! She was my friend. So, when I said, "Really, so-and-so? Did you really just say that? You really should think about what you are about to say before you say it; otherwise, you will sound ridiculous like you just have!" Cringe! That wasn't debating! That was disparaging, defaming, and insulting her! As soon as the words left my tongue, I wished I had not said them. My words and tone hurt her heart and broke her spirit. I saw it on her face. The remainder of the night, I was quiet from shame, and she was quiet from hurt. The next day I tried calling her to apologize for my bad behavior, but she would not take my call. When I unexpectedly showed up at her house, I found her in her bed, curled up in a fetal position. She was very surprised to see me as I rushed to the side of the bed and knelt there. She had been very sad and angry with me. I apologized and told her I was way out of line and that I would never treat her in such a horrible way again. I cried, and she simply said, "Khris, words can hurt." I not only hurt her feelings, but I also broke the trust she had in me to treat her with respect and kindness. She was right. Words can hurt.

That day, I vowed to guard my words with God's Word so that I could not intentionally hurt anyone with my words again. Sure, there will be times when people will be hurt by what you say, but if you are unintentionally using words badly, you're genuinely sensitive to their feelings, and you filter what you say by asking the Father to guard your tongue, you can speak confidently knowing you are not trying to hurt anyone. When we intentionally hurt those closest to us and strangers as well, we take their power; we are fighting unfairly. And isn't it our goal to empower one another so that we join forces in breaking down the strongholds of this world? Isn't it? Girls, we are charged with being changemakers.

"Let no unwholesome word proceed from your mouth, but only such a word as is good for edification according to the need of the moment, so that it will give grace to those who hear" (Ephesians 4:29).

Blasphemy can refer to harsh speech against God, sacred things, or sacred people. Those were ways, in biblical times, people committed blasphemy. Also, when Jesus performed miracles, people were so aghast that they were sure it was actually Satan working in the moment to make a lame man walk or a blind man to see. They couldn't believe Jesus, as a man walking this earth, could do such things! During Bible times attributing the miracles of Jesus to Satan was committing blasphemy. However, today, as the meaning has evolved, you can commit blasphemy when you speak things that are not true about another person. Be careful not to repeat something about another person someone has told you. It's really quite easy to fall victim to talking about other people disparagingly. It's always a good idea when you find the conversation going in that direction to steer it another way.

Evil speaking is similar to blasphemy in that it, too, disparages another individual's character, "putting someone down." If you have committed your heart to live for Jesus, the Holy Spirit will always warn you against engaging in such behavior. Always. That warning will be a feeling of uncomfortableness or guilt, or sometimes it is a still, small voice telling you what you are about to say should not be said.

Both of those sins of the tongue oftentimes begin with the third sin of the tongue: whispering. If you are not sitting in church, at the symphony, or any type of concert or recital requiring you to whisper, then whispering is wrong. Whispering implies that you are about to say something negative, disparaging, and evil, mostly about another person or situation. What do you think when you see one person whispering into the ear of another person? I always think what's being said is not appropriate enough for everyone to hear it.

When you complain, murmur, grumble, or gripe, God is displeased. The apostle Paul commands Christians to "do all things without grumbling and disputing" (Philippians 2:14). Who wants to be around a person who is complaining all the time? Complaining, grumbling, murmuring, and griping say about a person that they are unhappy, dissatisfied, and hard to please. Remember we are supposed to look like the image of Jesus. When Jesus lived on earth, He never complained, murmured, grumbled, griped, spoke ill of anyone, whispered about anyone, or blasphemed anyone. In fact, Jesus never sinned. He was and is today perfect. You are to live in pursuit of mirroring His character. No one on earth will ever be perfect! But when you aspire to change the negative characteristics of speaking, you not only benefit, but the message you are carrying across the world to girls like you is one bathed in building, not destroying.

## Wearing Emeralds

Take a moment to think back on a time you have taken part in any of these offenses of the tongue. How did it make you feel at the time?

In the space provided below, make a commitment to God that you will no longer participate in using your tongue to say things that destroy.

_____

_____

_____

_____

_____

_____

_____

_____

_____

_____

_____

_____

_____

_____

_____

_____

_____

_____

## Word Power

Eloquent: *Fluent or persuasive in speaking or writing.*

Write the name of the person in the space below who you know and would describe as eloquent.

Now explain why you think this person is eloquent.

_____

_____

_____

_____

_____

_____

_____

_____

_____

_____

_____

_____

_____

_____

_____

_____

_____

_____

Pam Case
For Ashley

*"Your loving, big heart, your directness, your realness, your sense*
*of humor, your thoughtfulness, your work ethic, your love of*
*travel, your yearning to be the best version of you is what makes*
*your essence! Always stay true to you."*

# CHAPTER 17

# Your Essence

*Girl*

I love words! I like to play with words, and I like to study their roots, origins, and meanings. For the last twenty years or so, I have won first place in the local Scrabble championship. Okay! Okay! Okay! Local to the Ferland household. No one can beat me. It gets old winning all the time, but what's a winner to do?

I love the sound of words in different languages, and when the meaning of a word jibes with the beauty of its look and sound, I really love that word! With my daughters and husband, I like to play around with the pronunciation of words to get a rise out of them, and they fall victim to it every time. One such word is the word "essence." I'll pronounce it with a French twist, like *es-sanz*. It just sounds so pretty that way!

What has the word essence to do with you?

Dear Daughter, every part of your journey to your destiny is enriched with the essence of who you are, giving you the girl power you need to navigate things on your path. But what is the essence of you? *Webster's New World Dictionary* says *essence* is "that which makes something what it is; intrinsic, fundamental nature or most important quality (of something); essential being." Another version says *essence* is "the inward nature of anything, underlying its manifestations, true substance." Yet another says *essence* is "one that has or shows an abundance of a quality as if highly concentrated."

*Essence* describes the heart of you coming alive in the different circumstances of your life contributing to you being you. I have a friend who, if I had to choose one word to describe her, her essence, the word would be *virtuous*, meaning moral excellence. She brings that virtue into everything. We have been in a lot of circumstances together, and no matter the time, place, or circumstance, she thinks, speaks, and acts virtuously. When she's angry, sad, or annoyed, her virtue shines through. No. She is not perfect; no one is. But she is striving to be with the ideals and principles of her relationship with God at the root. Again. Is she perfect? No. But the essence of her is virtuous, something to be deeply admired.

What I just did in describing my friend's essence, we should all want someone to describe our essence as so. Here's the thing, though. The essence of a person can be good or bad. You want someone to describe your essence in a positive light, describing the good nature of you. What do you think the essence of a person who lies all the time is? And the essence of a person who talks disparagingly about others is? And what's the essence of a person who is always negative and mean toward others? What's the essence of a person who always tries to control situations by manipulation?

How do you think the essence of a person evolves? Certainly, it does over time, and it grows from various parts of ourselves. The different parts of your character create your essence. But, also, our essence evolves from learning about ourselves as we interact with others and with our environments and how to navigate those interactions. For example, if you never learn how to effectively resolve conflict without it escalating to levels beyond the situation's control, then the essence of you could be described as argumentative because it's practiced over and over, thus becoming a part of who you are. Conversely, if you do learn how to diffuse situations that can be volatile, practicing calmness and ways to bring harmony, the essence of you could be described as a peacemaker. You can choose to nurture the good-natured essence of you and choose to irradicate the undesirable essence of you.

The moment God thought of you and began creating you, He envisioned you as a girl. A girl whose essence would develop to mirror Him. He didn't second guess Himself; He had no doubt about what He was doing, He was not confused, and He didn't make a mistake. You were indeed created to be a girl. Genesis 1:27 tells us, "So God created man in his own image, in the image of God he created him; male and female he created them." This verse is abundantly clear as to God's intention in creating you and everyone else, though our society will have you believe otherwise.

The purpose for creating mankind was for each of us to work together to advance the kingdom of God. All the physical characteristics God used to create you were to only create you, not anyone else. Sure, you and twenty of your closest friends may all have brown hair, but your brown hair is uniquely yours and is undoubtedly a different color brown than your friend's. You may have 2,521 strands of hair, while your friend may have 4,699 strands. Matthew 10:30 says, "But even the hairs on your head are all numbered." The detail with which God chose your hair, skin, eyes, and lips is uniquely yours, and no one on earth is exactly the same as you, even if you are identical twins! Really. Sometimes identical twins will have slightly different skin tones, weights, heights, and definitely personalities. I do not know what God was doing with that! But no one is even close to being uniquely you.

Do you understand the love and detail God used to make you who you are? Surely it must make your heart glad and bring a smile to your face once you understand that you were intentionally created. Everything about your physical appearance, heart, mind, and soul makes you who you are: a girl whose essence is evolving into positive attributes.

> "Before I formed you in the womb I knew you, and before you were born I consecrated you; I appointed you a prophet to the nations."
>
> Jeremiah 1:5

As so, your essence evolving allows for the possibility of it taking its root in the character of the Father. What role do you play in this?

1.  First, learn the nature and character of who God is by delving into His Word, the Bible. On every page, you will find Him.
2.  Emulate His character. Love like He loves, forgive like He forgives, and encourage as He does. Seek to be like Him.
3.  Always look for opportunities to identify things in your character to improve. (But don't be hard on yourself because that's what the enemy wants.)

Remember the enemy's job is to bring confusion and discord. First Peter 5:8 states, "Be of sober spirit, be on the alert. Your adversary, the devil, prowls around like a roaring lion, seeking someone to devour." Being sober-minded means to dwell in God's presence. When you dwell in God's presence, you are worshipping, praying, spending time alone with Him, and praising Him.

Daughters, the beauty that is birthed when you dwell in the presence of God is you being confident in who you are and embracing the direction God has for your life.

Imagine a car flying through the sky and an airplane driving on a six-lane freeway. Or a turtle is able to run as fast as a gazelle, and a gazelle is only able to move slowly, inching along as a turtle does. A turtle doesn't need to be able to move quickly. When a predator is lurking, the turtle protects itself by retracting its head, arms, and legs inside the shell of its exterior. For food, it eats bugs, which travel slowly, even slower than the turtle. The gazelle, on the other hand, was created with the ability to run at least fifty miles per hour! Although its source of food is mainly grass, the gazelle is preyed upon by all major predators in the ecosystem: lions, cheetahs, leopards, crocodiles, jackals, African wild dogs, hyenas, and humans. So God created the gazelle with the ability to move swiftly to avert predators to survive! God's divine purpose for things is His divine purpose, not ours. So you are charged with being who God created you to be, not who the enemy is telling you to be. He wants to destroy you and other girls like you so that you will not fulfill God's divine purpose for your life.

Sometimes we meet people who desire to be the opposite sex in which they are created. Just because we are different, does that mean we are to ostracize, alienate, or degrade those who are different from who we are? No! Do you hate people wanting to change the color of their hair or someone who lost a limb or someone who can't see or hear? No! God created everyone the way He expected us to live our purpose on earth, male or female. Does everyone believe this? Unfortunately, no.

Often, society will encourage us to hate those who have chosen to gender identify with whichever sex they choose. Hate is destructive, unsettling, divisive, crude, and diabolical. God has nothing to do with hate. Remember our goal as girls is to live righteously before the world so that they can come into their own relationship with God based on how we love and live. In so doing, you are contributing who you are—empowered, intelligent, and formidable young women—to a world desperately in need of what you have to give. Your essence.

Girl! You are amazingly beautiful. You were created to do beautiful things to help with building the kingdom of God. Your value to this earth is remarkable! Your physical toughness, ambition, and ability to take direction say you are a great athlete. Your willingness to serve others, intelligence, and staying power say you could run your own company. The fact that you are poised and a great communicator who isn't afraid to speak her mind and how you love debating the latest news and dismantling your opponent's views say you are an attorney. Your compassion for the wounded says you're a doctor. The creativity with which you come alive says you are a future novelist, designer, model, or actor. You are talented beyond what you know. Your voice is lovely; your heart is pure. Your ideas are respected, and your thoughts are valuable. You are strong, formidable, steadfast, and unmovable. You are important and adored. Take joy in being the girl God made you. Girl-empowered! Allow that to be the essence of you.

## Wearing Emeralds

Try describing your essence.

Now think of your closest friend and describe his or her essence the same way I described my friend's essence.

_____

_____

_____

_____

_____

_____

_____

_____

_____

_____

_____

_____

_____

_____

_____

_____

_____

_____

_____

_____

## Word Power

Girl: *A female, a young or relatively young woman.*

List reasons why you enjoy being a girl.

_____

_____

_____

_____

_____

_____

_____

_____

_____

_____

_____

_____

_____

_____

_____

_____

_____

_____

_____

_____

_____

_____

Rhonda Williams
For Michaela

*"Sometimes you have to fight for what you know, for what's right. Sometimes being a girl means being a warrior. You're not just a girl; you're a warrior. Your strength will carry you. Your God will keep you. Fight like a girl warrior."*

## CHAPTER 18

# Your Armor

*Complete*

Dear Daughter, have there been times in your life when you've felt like there was always a battle you need to fight? A fire to put out? Perhaps even now, you're feeling that you have just finished one battle, and another has already begun. Warrior girl, is the handle of your sword nearly broken from all of the swipes and swinging blows you've taken at the circumstances of your life? Is your arm tired from having taken so many swings? Your heart broken? Your emotions on a roller coaster ride? Or are you thinking that nothing turns out right for you? That no matter how much you try, you just don't seem to be able to get ahead of things. I won't tell you not to feel sad or discouraged by that because just battling the day-to-day occurrences of our lives is exhausting and can be discouraging if we perceive ourselves as being defeated. But I will tell you how to overcome this.

There comes a time in each of our lives when we experience this very thing that overwhelms our lives and causes us to question why all these attacks are coming against us. What is this about? What does it mean, and what are you supposed to do about it? Before I answer those questions, let me give you a little background on how I handled being whelmed by the circumstances of life when I was your age and how I handle it now. Two starkly different ways.

I'm not sure if I've mentioned it yet, but I'm a preacher's kid. And when I was your age, it was tough growing up as a preacher's kid. I feel such compassion and empathy for preachers' kids, especially when they're young. It seems like there is always something going wrong, something to wreak havoc on our lives. We feel like we live under a microscope, so we try to always be on our best behavior, always saying the right thing, doing the right thing, and going to the right places, having the right friends. Preachers' kids are expected by society to wear righteousness like a badge of honor, never to be taken off. And the handles of our swords are nearly broken from all the swipes and swings. It's seemingly not fair to preachers' kids that it's tough enough trying to grow through the different growth and development milestones and then having to do it with what feels like the world looking on. Why does it seem like we get a greater measure of attacks on our lives? Well, just like yours, our destinies are great. But part of a preacher's kid's destiny is laced with legacy. We are sometimes charged with having the mantle placed on our parents' lives to permeate our own lives, carrying the torch, so to speak. The attacks come like a lightning bolt across our lives.

So, when I was your age and experienced what seemed like nothing in my life going the way I would have liked and ten things going wrong at once, I felt hopeless, defeated, and like my life was falling apart. I became a rebel and acted in ways that could have cost me the beautiful future I didn't know was waiting. If that is you now, please know your life is not falling apart. It's actually falling together with pieces that seem shattered and broken but, in actuality, are pieces that, if recognized as a piece of an eventual beautiful whole, can be seen as valuable to you and will reveal your next steps on the path to your designed destiny. Those arduously ugly pieces fit perfectly together. You're thinking how failing one of the biggest exams of your academic career, not getting asked to the biggest school dance, wrecking your new car, fighting with your absolute best friend, all could be anything other than your world falling apart. Here's why it only feels like your world is falling apart and is really not. And I certainly am not negating the authenticity of unfortunate things happening to you, things that interrupt your life and, therefore, your peace. I'm simply saying that the culmination of all these things is not the end of your story. It is, in fact, an opportunity for you to grow by deciding to fight past what is happening. Once you decide to fight, you ask for help to fight, and your victory is guaranteed! Oh, how I wish at your age someone had told me that I had to fight and had taught me the smart way to do it.

The way I fight now is by ensuring that I am fully clothed with the armor I need to win.

Interestingly, as a girl your age, I never learned about the armor we are equipped with to fight those attacks. But I know about it now, and I use it every day. So, when it seems that everything is converging on you at once and you see no way out, it means that you are under a direct attack by the enemy. The enemy is a spirit that injects itself into situations in our lives with the purpose of causing discord and defeat. The discord that erupts across our lives is designed to prevent us from learning who we really are so that we never live the destiny God designed.

I know; I know; I know! That sounds so odd and far-fetched for some of you. It sounds crazy as I read it back to myself with the heart and mind of a girl your age. You, instead, may be inclined to believe that life just happens and everything in our lives will not always go as planned. You may have learned that bad things happen to good people. And all of that is true, but God's Word is clear that we are in a battle. And the battle is a spiritual one. We're spirit beings. Ephesians 6:12 is clear, "For our struggle is not against flesh and blood, but against the rulers, against the powers, against the world forces of this darkness, against the spiritual forces of wickedness in the heavenly places."

You: "Wait! Khris, what you're saying sounds crazy! Spirits? Darkness? Really?"

Me: "Girl, yes! I didn't make this stuff up, and it didn't originate with me! I just repeated what the Bible said. And remember you either believe *all* of the Bible or none of it. I suggest all. But let's break this down. Let's go just on the cusp of deep for you to understand. Just the cusp!"

Paul is writing this letter to the Christians of Ephesus, the Ephesians, warning them that the battles they would face are of a spiritual nature and the only way that they would be able to win is to fight in the spirit. Oh my! What does that mean? Keep reading.

As Christians we are in a continual battle, one that we typically never realize. The battle is to capture our lives, and the ultimate way to do this is to infiltrate our minds and spirits with a distorted view of who society says we are rather than what God says.

So the circumstance you can't seem to change, the problem you can never solve, the person you repeatedly have arguments with, the Bible says are caused by spirits working against the Spirit of God in you.

But there is profoundly good news, girls! We have an arsenal of tools to use to fight these battles and to give us the win in the end. Tools you don't know you have are readily accessible to you. You don't have to purchase them, barter for them, or borrow them. They're already waiting for you to begin to use them. God designed them for you to be successful against the attacks that come against your life.

> "Finally, be strong in the Lord and in the strength of His might. Put on the full armor of God, so that you will be able to stand firm against the schemes of the devil."
>
> Ephesians 6:10–11

In order to be successful in fending off these attacks against your life, you must first decide that you will fight. I'm noting that it is difficult to decide to fight what is happening to you when you feel your world is irreparably broken. But if you can, for a moment, step outside of your emotions and encourage yourself to fight, you will be glad you did. Empowering yourself with the knowledge on how to win and utilizing armor that was prepared for you should make the decision to fight easier when you're in a moment of despair.

Paul says to the Ephesians and to us, in addition to praying, you should clothe your spirit with six things; the "tools" I previously mentioned are your armor. Girl, these six things you must learn to fight with will not only design your win against the attacks but will also transform your relationship with God, give you the knowledge on how you approach different situations, and empower you to navigate your life spiritually. These tools are the belt of truth, the breastplate of righteousness, the shoes of peace, the shield of faith, the helmet of salvation, and the sword of the Spirit.

Before we get into the different pieces of armor that will frame how you fight against the enemy's attacks, take a moment to visualize a Roman soldier and what he looks like before going to war. He's fully clothed in armor that will help him be effective in winning the battle and protecting his life. Look at everything they wore. Each piece protects a part of the body, beginning at the head and cascading down to the feet.

We know what would happen if the soldiers did not wear all this armor. Guaranteed defeat. Why do you think we experience defeat when we are attacked in the circumstances of our lives? Because we don't wear the armor available to us. And how can we wear it if we don't know what it is?

You need to ensure this armor is at your disposal each day because 1 Peter 5:8 states that you should "be alert and sober-minded, your enemy the devil roams the earth seeking whom he may devour." You, of course, will never see him, but he and his demons are wreaking havoc in our lives through the spiritual realm. Oh! I know it all sounds crazy, but it is real! This is not a cause to be afraid of because you will always be victorious if you wear the spiritual armor God has provided for you. You are a warrior girl who is ready to recognize the battle, prepare for it, and win it!

The belt of truth represents knowledge and wisdom that emanates from God. Lately, the culture is encouraging you to "live your truth." The truth the culture encourages refers to an individual's personal belief system. If that belief system does not draw from the foundation of God's Word, then it is a blatant lie. That is a very bold, definitive, and absolute posture to have, I know, but He is the only truth. You are to use God's Word as a standard to measure everything concerning your life. If something does not align with what God's Word says, then it is a lie. In cultures where each individual has his own authority, when no one acknowledges or respects rules of authority, chaos ensues. That chaos transfers from our personal lack of acknowledgment of God's authority to our relationships, families, communities, and ultimately our world.

The breastplate of righteousness is how you will respond to what God says about the situations before you. What choices will you make? What actions will you take? Will you disregard His standard when making those choices, or will you submit? Submitting to His standard is you reacting righteously. In order to effectively use the breastplate of righteousness, you must already be wearing the belt of truth. Righteousness is the overflow of and natural progression of truth. It is the desire to live truth despite distractions designed to cause you to fall. If truth in you is distorted, it is impossible for you to enact righteous behavior.

The shoes of peace give you the calm you need in the midst of the storm in your life. How will you react to a situation—calmly or out of control, lacking the depth required to stand firm? Look at the feet of the Roman soldier in the picture above. He's wearing sandals! How can he protect his feet by wearing sandals! What we can't see is that those sandals have nails on the soles of them. Those nails enabled the soldier to stand firmly, not to be knocked off his feet. The nails gave him the footing he needed to stand strong and tremendously adept to win. When these soldiers wore those nails on their sandals, I'm sure they felt confident that they would not be pushed down. That's peace enabling them to fight more effectively. Paul is instructing us to shod our feet with the shoes of peace so that at any blowing of the wind or shove against us, we stand firm trusting in the nails of peace on the bottoms of our shoes. When the negative circumstances of life come to destroy us, we are to protect our peace by planting our feet solidly and firmly and knowing that if we do, victory is imminent. So many times, things will happen in our lives to steal our peace. Your mind races with thoughts of defeat in whatever battle you are fighting. But if you can dig your feet in deeply to grasp peace, you can win.

The shield of faith enables you to continue to walk forward in the direction God is leading despite what you feel because you are trusting the Father to help. I can remember times in my life when faith was hard to grasp. There will be times in your life that will require you to have faith as being the only way you can and will win in a situation. You won't always need faith for everything. My refrigerator is filled with food. Tonight, when it's time for me to eat dinner, will I need to have faith that I'll have something to eat? No. I recently applied to a university whose acceptance rate is 10 percent to obtain a graduate degree. Sure, I met the basic requirements, but twenty-two thousand people apply to this university's graduate program, and only twenty-two hundred are accepted each year. Did I need to have faith for a positive outcome? Yes! Faith rooted in God's plan for me.

Take another look at the picture of the Roman soldier and how he holds the shield across his body. He is trained and ready to adjust the position of the shield in a moment's notice to shield his face, then to move it across his chest area, and then across his torso and legs. In battle it will be moved across his body and held to fend off the advances of his opponent throughout the battle. This is for you too. You will need to use that shield of faith sometimes, and sometimes you won't need it. But don't allow your faith to collect dust when you don't need it. During this time, gather up the shield and prepare it to serve you for when you will need it. This means seeking the Word of God, reading it with expectancy, and meditating on the verses so that when you are in a battle, your shield of faith is ready to help you win.

The helmet of salvation is covering your mind with the knowledge of God and protecting it from evil and negative thoughts the enemy puts there to cause you to stumble. He designed these thoughts to play over and over in your mind so that you become afraid and incapacitated. Your mind is the focal point of everything about you and is where your thoughts rest. You have the power and authority to decide what rests there. The foremost thought that should rest in your mind and be protected by the helmet of salvation is that you are loved with a love that is unconditional and unending, complete and encompassing, and dependable and trustworthy. That love covers anything you will ever endure and gives you a victory that is guaranteed. When you can protect that thought, you are wearing your helmet of salvation.

The sword of the Spirit is the Word of God. You won't know the extent of its power until you see it come alive in a moment that is overpowering you. When you speak the Word over the circumstances of your life, walls fall, mountains move, things are restored to you, and change happens. The key to using the Word of God over the moments of your life is to be prepared. Scriptures you have ready to say and meditate on when the attacks of the enemy come. The only way that you can be ready is to meditate on the Scripture, store it in your heart and mind, and deliver it when you need. You will be surprised at how empowered you feel after having unleashed God's Word onto a situation consuming your life. Practicing this will become commonplace to you and will transform your perspective on the battles you face. You will expect to win the battles in your life.

Daughter, using these six pieces of armor coupled with an active prayer life will bring about the change in your life you are seeking. A good way to practice "putting on" the armor of God is to plan. Each morning when you awake just before your feet hit the floor, put on the belt of truth by making a gesture to put on a belt. As you are putting the belt of truth around your waist, make a vow to measure everything you face that day by what God's Word says on the matter. For example, say, "God, as I put on my belt of truth, I will acknowledge Your truth in everything I do today." Then make the gesture of putting on the breastplate of righteousness, again vowing to respond to circumstances of your day the way God's Word says you should. You will put on each piece of armor this way until you are ready for your day. The extra five to ten minutes will serve you well. When you consistently do this and practice the principles of each piece of armor, you will begin to experience greater victory in your life. You will.

Each piece of armor provides a specific characteristic the Holy Spirit enhances your life with. Together, as a whole, this armor empowers you sixfold to win the wars waged against you; those times it seems nothing is going right in your life, and you are experiencing one unfortunate thing after the other.

It's direly important to use this armor to your advantage; otherwise, the enemy will regularly cause destruction in your life, and he will win! But once you make a practice of spiritually donning your armor, his reign in your life ends, and you emerge as the warrior God intended you to become.

I remember growing up as a child often watching television and seeing one of the best advertisement campaigns for American Express credit cards. You're much too young to remember it or have seen it. The commercial showed consumers experiencing an exceptional life because of the credit card as they navigated day-to-day circumstances. The underlying message was that the card added such extreme value to their lives and made things so much easier for them. The clincher was, "Don't leave home without it!" The commercial implied that the credit card's use was so invaluable and so convenient to consumers that the consequences of being without it would be great. Girl, likewise, for your armor. You cannot leave home without it!

## Wearing Emeralds

List the six pieces of armor in the space below and write what you will say each morning when putting on your armor to indicate the purpose of each piece of armor.

_____

_____

_____

_____

_____

_____

_____

_____

_____

_____

_____

_____

_____

_____

_____

_____

_____

_____

_____

## Word Power

Complete: *Having all the necessary and appropriate parts; to the greatest extent or degree.*

God says you are complete because you are His daughter and heir. Do you think you are complete? Why or why not?

_____

_____

_____

_____

_____

_____

_____

_____

_____

_____

_____

_____

_____

_____

_____

_____

_____

_____

Vanessa Van Trease
For Isabella

*"Fear of failure builds walls that separate us from the truth and the promises the Lord has bestowed upon our lives. To break through, trust in His promises. His promises are scriptures. Recite them aloud and watch as the walls of your fear of failure crumble."*

## CHAPTER 19

# Your Failures

*Brave*

Dear Daughter, failure has the potential to wield a power on your life so great if, after you've not received an anticipated outcome, you resign. Quit. Give up. Walk away. Have you ever been disappointed at your performance on something you've attempted? Produced less favorable results on a test that determined your next steps in life? Do you think it's your fault that the relationship ended? What have you attempted, and the result was not a successful outcome for you, the outcome you were expecting? What are you afraid of trying?

I can't count the number of times I spearheaded projects that were not successful, tests I took that I didn't pass, and made wrong decisions that caused me to stumble. I've also allowed overwhelming thoughts to prevent me from initiating either something required of me or something I desired to do.

Everyone in the universe has failed many times in their lives. And so will you. Our failing is characterized in three ways.

1. Attempting a task but producing an unfavorable, unanticipated, and negative outcome.
2. Not attempting a task because of fear of producing an unfavorable, unanticipated, and negative outcome.
3. Not attempting a task because of lack of motivation.

These are all forms of failing. The most relatable and most common times we fail is when we engage in something either required of us or initiated on our own, and for whatever reason the outcome was not deemed successful. This causes a gamut of emotions we feel, and the strength to move forward is weak. Shame, discouragement, bewilderment, and hopelessness cause delays in trying again. What happens next can be a defining moment for your future. I know when you feel you have failed, the mental energy you need to move forward is lacking. You cannot find it. Helping you decide and determine your next step after experiencing failure is what this chapter is about. If you learn the aforementioned characteristics of failure, practice the concepts listed when you do stumble, and you will be empowered to see the value in failing. So, when your efforts have produced an outcome that seems unpromising, the key here is to gather, collect, and glean as much information from the process of the effort you extended. This is extracting the value from the failure. I believe there is value in any failure.

For example, if you have ever failed a math test, a good teacher will insist you rework the problems you completed wrong. What this enables is that you don't move to the next concept without knowing the correct way to perform the problems you worked incorrectly. Why is it so important to do this? It is vitally important to thoroughly learn one concept before moving to the next because one math concept builds on the next. You need the information from one concept to effectively learn the new concept. Such is the case when you fail at job performance, relationships, a project you undertake. It is vitally important that you learn from your shortcomings first, use the information that caused you to be unsuccessful, and that you try a different approach that ensures a successful outcome is the result the next time.

I remember a time when what I thought was the biggest failure turned out to be the biggest value to my life. This failure changed the trajectory of my life as I had planned it, causing me tremendous disappointment and apathy. I withdrew from who I was.

Years ago, as a post-high school graduate, it was very important to my mother that I became a nurse, despite my heart being set on becoming a journalist. She knew that nurses always had jobs and could take great care of themselves quite soon after obtaining a nursing degree. Whereas journalists spend several years building a career after graduating college. So off I went to nursing school. I actually did quite well; having been an honors student in high school, I was prepared for the grueling curriculum nurses undergo. However, after graduating from nursing school, nurses take an exam to obtain a license to practice. Well, I was one of only two classmates who failed the nursing board exam! I was devastated! I felt like the biggest failure and was so ashamed that I didn't leave my home for several days and definitely didn't accept consolation calls from my friends. My heart was filled with the same measure of torture and affliction my head was housing. Because when you think you've failed, it's a type of pain that resonates loudly in the mind. There was nothing that would make me try taking the exam again. I quit the nursing profession feeling defeated and ashamed and rationalized that it wasn't my passion anyway. I then went on to obtain another degree in broadcast journalism and a successful career as a news anchor and reporter. However, through the years I always felt I wasted so much of my time and my parent's money in nursing school. That "failure" haunted me for years.

Then one day, many years later, a couple of decades in fact, Kierstin, Kerrigan, and I were playing "monster" in the family room of our home, a silly game the girls always played sometimes after Kierstin's school day. Routinely, Kierstin assigned herself to be the monster, and I was Kerrigan's protector, shielding her from being captured. We had just returned from the Valentine's Day party at Kierstin's school, and she, no doubt, was full of all the sugar she had collected as candy. Kierstin was six, and Kerrigan was almost two. The game would start with Kierstin pretending to frighten her sister with the horrendous sound of a big, bad monster, and Kerrigan would run laughing hysterically into my waiting arms. There was something so sweet about Kerrigan's laughter that caused Kierstin and I to double over in laughter as well. After minutes of watching the two play, I scooped up Kerrigan and turned, shielding her from Kierstin to take her to another room to get her washed and comfortable for her afternoon nap. As I turned, I felt the worst pain travel down the center of my back as if Kierstin had taken her baseball bat and hit me with it. But I didn't remember seeing the baseball bat in the family room, though my husband and I often took turns reprimanding her for bringing it into the family room from the garage. The pain was so penetrating that I almost collapsed to the floor with Kerrigan in my arms but mustered the energy to stay afoot. When I turned to reprimand Kierstin, I saw her gripping her throat, unable to breathe! Her face was red, her lips were blue, and she had fallen to her knees. She hadn't been making monster sounds at all! The sound I heard mimicking fake monster sounds was her struggling to breathe. And she hadn't hit me with a baseball bat; the Holy Spirit had so that I could turn to see my girl choking. I immediately dropped Kerrigan, and I gathered Kierstin up into my arms, placing my hands in a cupping position underneath her rib cage. Exactly the way I had learned the Heimlich maneuver in nursing school. With each thrust of my cupped hands, I pleaded with God to help me save my girl! With the first thrust underneath her sternum, the yelping sent waves of anger to the base of my throat, and I cried out. The second thrust was me shunning the idea of calling 911 because I didn't want to risk wasting time. And the third thrust was me crying out the name of Jesus, the Master of the universe, the Great and Mighty I Am. Then, the biggest piece of candy I had ever seen in my life popped out of Kierstin's mouth. She began coughing and gasping, which signaled to me she would be okay. I began to cry as all the times I had felt ashamed, sad, embarrassed, and worthless about having failed my nursing licensing exam came back to my mind in that very moment. You see, my favorite part of the nursing program I was enrolled in was the week my friends and I learned the Heimlich maneuver! It was a week of fun and practicing on my classmates, skipping our regular courses to learn this gem that would frame a defining moment in my life. Yes! All those years ago, God knew that I was a broadcast journalist by gifting, but He allowed me to graduate from the nursing program because I would need to make a big piece of candy travel back up my daughter's throat so that she could live! That was me possessing the value of a failure I had experienced decades prior. God will give you the value in what you believe is failure!

Failure is also when we allow the fear of attempting something new to prevent us from trying. We talked about fear and how it can literally incapacitate us in an earlier chapter. There are so many things I am doing now in my latter life that I was too afraid to attempt when I was your age. I lived in fear of failure because I worried about what other people would think if I wasn't successful. It's a wonderful time in your life when you decide that despite not attaining the desired outcome in a situation, it doesn't define you, nor does it mean the end of who you are. It means you are growing. You are not defined by your failures but by what you do after you have failed. You will not be successful at everything you attempt. In fact, do you know that sometimes God Himself designs your unsuccessfulness to teach you valuable lessons on your journey to destiny? He also allows you to be what we describe as unsuccessful to show you that because you have decided to live righteously, as a Christian, you will always overcome. Always. He delights in showing Himself to you in ways you can't imagine in your failures.

Lack of mental thoughtfulness or motivation is a form of failure too. When a person's lack of mental motivation is not attributed to mental illness but is attributed to being lackadaisical or lazy, that person is failing themselves and wasting their valuable time. Mental laziness is not setting goals, not dreaming about your future, not thinking about and planning for what I call the next level of who you are.

Sometimes the motivation to try something new is met with so many distractions that are seemingly more attractive than trying at something you're not sure will succeed. It's downright daunting! That's when the self-talk and encouragement you learned in a previous chapter will come in handy. Talk yourself up, girl! You're going to win. You just don't know it yet.

Remember when we talked about victory? I stated that Jesus' death and then victory on the cross were also given to us as believers. We will always be victorious during the process of arriving at a failure, in challenges and trials. I always say our victory is guaranteed. Always. Knowing this should make you feel empowered to live your life confidently and boldly.

Guaranteed victory is what God defines as your victory, which could look quite different than what you were hoping the outcome would be because when we trust Him with our lives, He ensures the best thing for our lives. Go back to the story of how I completed nursing school, failed the board exam, decided to change professions, and went on to have a very successful career as a broadcast journalist. That was my victory guaranteed because God knew better than my mother and I that a part of my destiny was to become a news anchor, not a nurse.

God wants your faith in Him in any given situation to be greater than what your senses lead you to believe about the situation. Just because you feel like a failure does not mean you are. Don't be afraid to fail because you will learn lessons of truth about your relationship with God and yourself. Humans fail at things all the time, but as Christians we will always overcome our failures. Yes, it is very painful to find that you have failed after having devoted your time and talents to a project, a relationship, a sport, or an idea. It hurts because no one expects to fail; instead we expect to be successful in everything we commit to. But there is success in failure; success comes after what you think is failure if you persevere.

"When he falls, he will not be hurled headlong, Because the Lord is the One who holds his hand" (Psalm 37:24).

Failing is not you being deficient. Nor is it you not being good enough. It's you transforming into the next phase of beautiful you. Your failures are designed to make you grow and soar to the next level in you becoming the empowered young girl God created you to be. So, whenever you think you have failed, take notes on how you arrived to the place of what you are considering your failure, think about what you could have done differently, and move forward by putting the differences into practice. Remember what real failure is and what characterizes failing: trying but producing a less favorable outcome, allowing fear to prevent you from attempting something new, and lacking mental motivation to try. If you never fail at something, you will never grow at anything.

## Wearing Emeralds

Take a moment to think back on all the times in your life you think you failed at something. Write it down. Then, for every failure, think about the value that came from your failure. Write the value next to the failure, writing the word "but" before writing the value.

For example:

*I failed my nursing board exam, but the Heimlich maneuver I learned in nursing school helped me to save my daughter's life.*

_____

_____

_____

_____

_____

_____

_____

_____

_____

_____

_____

_____

_____

_____

_____

## Word Power

Brave: *Ready to face danger or pain, showing courage.*

Have you ever had to show bravery and courage during a difficult time? Describe it here. Be sure to write about how you overcame.

_____

_____

_____

_____

_____

_____

_____

_____

_____

_____

_____

_____

_____

_____

_____

_____

_____

_____

_____

Kecia Smalls
For Kailen

*"Resolve life's challenges, setbacks, and obstacles by using your spiritual compass as the navigational tool to help you derive the best solution for you. Rely on your faith, remain steadfast in your triumphs, and know that victory is birthed by conquering fear, apprehension, anxiety, and self-doubt."*

## CHAPTER 20

# Your Resolve

*Resolute*

Dear Daughter, resolve is another one of those words I really like because it, too, sounds like its meaning. It sounds strong, right? I searched and searched many dictionaries and did a few Google searches as well to find the meaning of *resolve* (for you) that best suits what I want you to learn from this chapter. My favorite dictionary puts it quite simply. Resolve is "to decide firmly on a course of action." Resolve. Isn't that a good word? I love its meaning!

Situations that require you to have great resolve are usually when you are seemingly out of options, your back is against a wall, doom is closing in on you, or the odds seem stacked against you. That is a tough spot to navigate because not only do you have to first decide you will get out of the situation causing you anxiety, but you also need to actually create a way out, as well as dig deep to muster the mental capacity to do so. Whew! That's tough. But keep reading.

You probably already have, or no doubt will, found yourself in a situation where you will need your determination so that you position yourself to win, to succeed, or to overcome a challenge or obstacle. And that determination will need to rise up inside of you greatly.

Do you remember Bethany Hamilton? She's a professional surfer who, at the age of thirteen, lost her arm to a shark attack as she was surfing one day. But returned to the waters a month later to continue her passion: to surf. She said, "I believe in Jesus Christ, and I believe He gave me the passion and determination to continue surfing. You fall off the horse, and you get back on. I had to go for it!" Her resolve to continue surfing competitively became greater than the fact that she had lost her arm. She was unwavering in her determination to continue engaging in a sport she loved. What does the flip side of that look like? Her having quit surfing, her God-given passion, gift, and talent. Never having surfed again? Not gone on to win numerous competitions? Not served as a courageous, determined young woman for you and girls like you?

You see, there are going to be roadblocks, mishaps, hardships, and disappointments, but determination in the midst of all this ignites your resolve. You may not feel strong enough to muster the courage and bravery it will take to persevere through a tough moment in your life. But remember, as girls ready to take on the world, we do not operate on feelings but on the faith that is given to you when having great resolve is an option.

"Do you not know that those who run in a race all run, but only one receives the prize? Run in such a way that you may win."

1 Corinthians 9:24

The only way you can win is if you participate in the race and persevere in the midst of challenges. Don't wait until the challenge is upon you to decide your course of action. Decide beforehand that on your journey and in the face of adversity, you will gather up all the courage, bravery, grit, and resolve to succeed at the task before you so that when the challenge comes, you just need the plan to overcome it. And remember you are never alone on your journey. When you are facing a giant, God will always work in your life if you commit your life to His will for your life. He will do the things you can't do. So sharpen your resolve and go for it!

You can always recognize someone who has a greater resolve by certain character traits. She is diligent, steadfast, earnest, bold, resolute, purposeful, and courageous. Just writing those words makes me feel empowered! Likewise, you can also recognize someone without resolve; she is wavering, indecisive, fearful, timid, lackadaisical, and questioning. How do your friends describe you, and how do strangers see you? Most importantly how do you see yourself, and how does God see you? The Bible speaks often about having resolve and how important it is if you're going to live a victorious Christian life in Jesus. I can think of two scenarios where you'll need to display great resolve.

1. When your response to a dire situation is being relied on by others for a greater good and time is not on your side. You'll need to think quickly, decide a course of action quickly, and execute quickly.
2.  You do have the luxury of time to plan your response and victory to a challenge you are facing. You have made a commitment to do the work required to have a successful outcome.

Sometimes you'll have the luxury of time to decide firmly on a course of action, and sometimes you won't. But understand the lack of the luxury of time does not mean you can't win or be successful. It simply means the situation requires a quick, under-the-gun response.

I think another all-time great display of "having a greater resolve" was during the 1996 Olympics. You are much too young to remember Kerri Strug. She was a part of the gymnastics Olympic team referred to as the Magnificent Seven, seven fierce and formidable young women seeking a team gold medal. The entire gymnastics event was a closely fought contest with standout Russian and Romanian teams. But we, in the US, liked to think that we indeed were favored to win, as the USA women's gymnastics team consisted of the best gymnasts in the world. And the US was leading going into the final event, the vault! I remember watching with sweet anticipation that the US was about to win yet another gold medal, and the Magnificent Seven would make history as the first US women's gymnastics team to ever win a team gold medal. It was electrifying to watch. Fourteen-year-old Dominique Moceanu, the youngest member of the team, was going to seal the win, as she was up first. But then, running powerfully up that runway, she fell. I thought, *That's okay; that's okay; she has another.* She fell on the second vault as well, and my heart sank for her, for the team. Tears swelled in my throat, and the agony of defeat took a seat in my heart and was comfortable there. It was Kerri Strug's turn to vault. Although Kerri was a phenomenal gymnast, she would have to perform the impossible under pressure, under scrutiny, and under the hope of failure from her opponents. After all, they, too, were in pursuit of the same gold medal. She would have to replace the negative voices in her head with positive ones. She would have to ignore the feeling of fear in her stomach and instead reach the feeling of being a lioness that lay in her gut. She would have to dig deep and find that place that had the courage and bravery she needed to get to a greater resolve. Kerri attempted the first vault and fell. Yes. She, too, fell. The gasps from hundreds of spectators still resonate in my mind today. Not only did Kerri fall, but she also realized she had injured her ankle as she got up and tried to walk. The world watched her wince in pain. I imagine in her mind it was a long walk down the vault runway limping on one ankle. It was over. But she was limping down the runway to get in position to perform her second vault! Wait! What? I sat there in the comfort of my childhood home despondent in heart for our USA Olympic team, and tears swelled my eyes this time as I tried looking at the bench of our girls the camera panned to. I immediately thought how courageous Kerri was to want to honor the moment and her team by performing her second vault although she was injured. It would still put points on the board for the US, and our team would continue to be respected in the gymnastics world despite the performance not measuring to gold status. I further rationalized the US's impending loss that many of us would have stopped at that point, and rightfully so. No shame in quitting when you're injured. But Kerri wanted to perform her second vault on an injured ankle. At that point she was already a hero in everybody's minds. She and Dominique and the entire team. And while we were thinking it was so honorable for Kerri to do her second vault although she was hurt, she was thinking, *I'm going to do this second vault and win the USA Women's Gymnastics Team their first team gold medal!* For what happened next, she had to be thinking that!

The cameras panned a close-up shot of Kerri's face just before she attempted the second vault; she was looking at her coach, Bella Karolyi. He was yelling, "Kerri, you can do it! Kerri, you can do it!" I thought to myself, sitting in my home, *Didn't he just see her limping? She's hurt! Enough is enough, Coach!*" But running up the runway to approach the vault, you could see this look on Kerri's face as she catapulted herself into the air and landed perfectly on an injured ankle but with a champion's heart. The crowd there erupted in shouts, laughter, and tears. Not only had Kerri dug deep to secure the team's gold medal, but she had also led her team to Olympic history!

Dear Daughter, decide and stand firmly with deep determination to do what God is urging you to do. Equip yourself with the courage, bravery, and mindset to persevere in the face of adversity despite something about you being broken. Your ankle may not be injured or broken; maybe it's your heart.

Maybe the thoughts about yourself are broken thoughts. Maybe your hopes and dreams are broken. Perhaps it's an idea or plan you made that's broken. Now is the time to decide to try your second vault with a greater resolve! Do it scared, do it hurt, do it wounded, do it broken. When you do, you will first see the Father, and then you will hear Him yelling to you, "Daughter, you can do it!"

## Wearing Emeralds

Take a moment to think about things in your past you wish you had persevered through. List those here. Afterward, promise the Father that, moving forward, you will commit to practicing a greater resolve in your relationship with Him and also in challenges you meet.

_____

_____

_____

_____

_____

_____

_____

_____

_____

_____

_____

_____

_____

_____

_____

_____

_____

_____

## Word Power

Resolute: *Admirably purposeful, determined, and unwavering.*

Is there a time or incident in your life that required you to be unwavering and determined, resolute, and you were? Describe it here.

_____

_____

_____

_____

_____

_____

_____

_____

_____

_____

_____

_____

_____

_____

_____

_____

_____

_____

Shanna Adams

For Lili

*"Things may not always go the way you thought or wished they would, but there is always something to be grateful for. If you start and end each day thinking about the things you are thankful for, you will wake up each morning and go to bed each night with a smile in your heart."*

## CHAPTER 21

# Your Thanksgiving

*Grateful*

Dear Daughter, what are you thankful for? Do you always remember to be thankful? Take a look at your life and recognize the beauty even if there are things that are not what you want them to be. What we forget is that there is always something to be thankful about despite things, circumstances, and people in our lives not being perfect. Oftentimes we're not thankful because we either forget the blessings we have, we take them for granted, or we don't see them as blessings at all. Oh, I'm sure you've heard it countless numbers of times, "There is so much to be thankful for." I certainly have, as a girl your age, heard my parents say to my siblings and me that very thing. Then they would proceed to break it down. Each breath you take, the home you live in, the clothes you wear, the food you eat, the test you passed, the amazing friend you have, your wonderful family are all blessings from the Almighty God we so easily take for granted.

It's easy to lose perspective of the life we are blessed to live as citizens of the United States of America. By biblical standards if we measure tangible things in our lives, compared to many other countries, the poorest individual living in the United States is rich. Socioeconomic status measures or assesses a person or family's access to resources based on their income, occupation, and education. A person's or family's socioeconomic status falls into one of three categories on that basis: high, middle, and low. Needless to say, typically those with the highest level of income, top-tiered occupations, and highest levels of education are at the highest socioeconomic status. Most celebrities are there too.

Certainly, when we see parts of the United States, we see poverty framed with homelessness, hunger, joblessness, and various other societal ills. But the United States is richer and better equipped than most countries to provide the resources its citizens need to grow past poverty. That, indeed, is something valuable to be thankful about—a country committed to fashioning and designing programs to relieve the burden of poverty from its citizens.

What if one day you decided to list all the things you're thankful for? What would that list look like? How long or short would it be? Trying to list everything you're thankful for is surely impossible. There is not enough time, not enough words to express, and certainly not enough patience to list everything. Let me tell you, as sure as the sky is limitless, you can never be thankful enough. What Jesus did for you can never be measured in terms of thankfulness; its scope is complex, and its depth is dimensionless. I think our lives and intentionally living them guided by the Word of God should be our thanksgiving to Jesus. I will tell you this: thankfulness always begins with Jesus. For if it were not for Jesus and His death on the cross, you would not have life the way Jesus fuels it.

You will find it interesting to learn what psychology says about gratitude and thankfulness. According to Positive Psychology,

> when we express gratitude and receive the same, our brain releases dopamine and serotonin, the two crucial neurotransmitters responsible for our emotions, and they make us feel "good." They enhance our mood immediately, making us feel happy from the inside. Positive psychology is the branch of psychology that uses scientific understanding and effective intervention to aid in the achievement of a satisfactory life, rather than merely treating mental illness.[3]

If that's not motivating enough to be thankful and show gratitude, I don't know what is. Do you see the connection? When God was creating our brains, He wired them so that when we express thankfulness and gratitude—He designed it to release a chemical that makes us feel good! So a perpetual cycle of feeling good and having peace and joy is created. Is that why the Bible is inundated with lessons on thankfulness! (I stopped counting after I found one hundred.) Wow! Here are a few of my favorites:

1. "Do not be anxious about anything, but in everything by prayer and supplication with thanksgiving let your requests be made known to God" (Philippians 4:6).
2. "Giving thanks always and for everything to God the Father in the name of our Lord Jesus Christ" (Ephesians 5:20).
3. "Oh give thanks to the Lord, for he is good, for his lovingkindness is everlasting" (Psalm 107:1).
4. "Whatever you do, in word or deed, do all in the name of the Lord Jesus, giving thanks to him through God the father" (Colossians 3:17).
5. "Rejoice always, pray without ceasing, in everything give thanks for this is God's will for you in Christ Jesus" (1 Thessalonians 5:16–18).

Sometimes as humans we forget to be thankful and grateful for life and the contents of our lives. We take for granted breathing when it is not guaranteed. You may be wondering how someone can forget to be thankful. Very easily. Remember it is the enemy's job to take your attention away from your relationship with God. He does not want you to train your thinking in a spirit of thankfulness because that will honor God. The enemy wants to capture your thoughts of God to distort them, sever your relationship with Jesus, and dismantle a bridge to thankfulness.

When I look back on a time in my life when I was your age, I see I didn't have the opportunity to learn about the importance of being thankful or showing gratitude. Yes. As mentioned a few sentences back, my parents often lectured my siblings and me about being grateful and thankful. The lecture on being grateful came when I wanted the pink bicycle, but I got an orange one. Or when I received a make and model of the car they bought for me, and it was not one I had asked for. But they were remiss in teaching the fact that I even received a bicycle or car at all was a blessing and something to be extraordinarily grateful for. There were two major things that contributed to my ungratefulness as a teen that you can ensure don't affect your ability to be thankful and show more gratitude.

1. I was always highlighting the negative, unable to see the good and beauty in things I received and challenging circumstances I found myself in. I never took the time to notice or learn the good thing that could have possibly come from the challenge.

2. I often compared myself and my things to those of my friends and acquaintances, often deciding whatever my friends had was categorically better than what I had. Oftentimes we focus our attentions on what we don't have rather than what we do have. In doing this, we are opening up ourselves to grow dissatisfied, envious, and covetous. It won't be long thereafter before we are comparing ourselves to someone else, further growing ungrateful for what we do have and wishing for what we don't have. Wherever you are on your journey in life, be assured and thankful that God has allowed you to be wherever you are for reasons you may not know now but will surely be revealed in God's time.

Though I was only a middle-to-high schooler, I wasn't too young to learn to be thankful and that if I did, it would serve me well in my adult life. And that's one thing I am extraordinarily grateful for and thankful about. I did not carry those negative things in my character into my adult life. Ungrateful, thankless girls grow into the same kind of women. That's why you're here, holding this book in your hands, learning things that will set you on course to benefit from being thankful.

I might add that I realize it's very difficult, when you are in the middle of a challenge, to not respond based on how you feel about the negative circumstance you're experiencing. The Bible tells us so eloquently to "walk by the Spirit so you will not carry out the desire of the flesh" (Galatians 5:16, NASB). You're to respond based on what the Word of God says about the situation, not based on how you feel. That is very difficult to do but not impossible. It's only difficult because humans tend to nurture their feelings, especially negative ones. Once you empower yourself with meditating on Bible scriptures and putting them in your heart, you are armed to be thankful instead of complaining, griping, and giving up when faced with a challenge. "Walking by the Spirit" means being in constant communication with God.

Daughter, we are encouraged to always be thankful, especially when we are challenged. I must reiterate the Bible verse in a few lines back, "Give thanks in all circumstances for this is the will of God in Christ Jesus for you." The reason God emphasizes thankfulness and gratitude is because thankfulness moves Him to act on your behalf. Also, a heart of thankfulness tells God that you know He is in control of everything, that you know He gave Jesus so that you may live, and that you are committing the details of your life to God. Being thankful tells God you trust Him.

> "Be anxious for nothing, but in everything by prayer and supplication with thanksgiving let your requests be made known to God. And the peace of God, which surpasses all understanding will guard your hearts and minds in Christ Jesus."
>
> Philippians 4:6–7

Be careful when reading the Bible verse above. It does not read, "In some things by prayer and supplication with thanksgiving." It does read, "In everything by prayer and supplication with thanksgiving." Paul is instructing you to be thankful no matter what challenge you are facing. When you are in a challenging circumstance and you feel you are losing, you are to begin to give thanks to God, not for the challenge but for the opportunity for God to intervene on your behalf and also for the opportunity to experience God on another level as He works things in your favor, becoming your victor. That's what thanksgiving is about. You are thanking Him because we know that "all things work for the good of those who love the Lord" (Romans 8:28). You are thanking Him because "greater is He that is in you than He who is in the world" (1 John 4:4). You are thanking Him because when "the righteous cry out the Lord hears and delivers them out of all their troubles. [He] is near to the broken hearted and [He rescues] those who are crushed in spirit" (Psalm 34:17). Developing a heart of gratitude and thanksgiving is vital to growing your relationship with God, yourself, and others.

Being thankful serves as a great witnessing tool to unbelievers. I remember an acquaintance of our family knew that I was experiencing a difficult period. I was baffled as to why God had allowed my contract to expire at a job I thought suited me well. When my acquaintance saw that I was not devastated, she became confused, for she knew how much I liked this particular job. As we spoke, I explained to her that I was thankful for my time there, that I had gotten the opportunity to gain valuable experience for the next opportunity surely God was sending my way. She asked, "How are you thankful for your contract not being renewed!" As I explained to her, it was easy. I knew I had done nothing wrong on the job and that God must have been moving me for a better opportunity. The thought of a better opportunity made my heart glad, and I was able to thank God before the next opportunity presented itself.

Daughter, thanksgiving is such a blessing to behold. It can fill your heart with gladness, hope, joy, and peace. Usually, I enter into thanksgiving in a quiet place as I praise and worship. The songs I play exalt the Father and bring glory to who He is. The songs bring me into His presence as I lift my hands and heart to glorify His majesty. I allow my mind to go to His throne as I imagine myself kneeling at His feet. Thanksgiving fills me. I thank Him for thinking I am worthy of Him, me belonging to Him. I thank Him for thinking I am beautiful, me actually being beautiful. I thank Him for being with me at every point of each day, me waking to see each day! Oh! There is so much to be thankful for! Commit to focusing on thanksgiving and watch your relationship with the Father go deeper and wider.

Once you make a practice of thanksgiving, you will begin to feel more joy and peace because what you're actually doing is reflecting on the details of your life and inviting God into them, and that's a wonderful thing, inviting God into the details of your life.

Here are a few things you can do to intentionally practice being more thankful:

1. Regularly assess what you say. When you interact with people, those you are and are not acquainted with, ensure that you are intentionally saying the words "thank you" followed by what you are thankful for when an act of kindness has been extended to you.

2. Identify and take note of your wins. Since we are so inclined to keep record of all the times we think we have failed ourselves, begin to keep record of the times you prevail. Write it down in a journal. Then thank yourself for the win. This will enable you to feel a sense of accomplishment and satisfaction with yourself in addition to birthing joy and happiness.

Practicing being grateful and thankful is a journey with rewards along the way. The best reward is the gift of peace you give yourself because you were kind enough to others when your heart filled with thankfulness.

## Wearing Emeralds

Use the space below to remind yourself of the importance of being thankful, then list a few things you are thankful for.

_____

_____

_____

_____

_____

_____

_____

_____

_____

_____

_____

_____

_____

_____

_____

_____

_____

_____

_____

## Word Power

Grateful: *Feeling or showing an appreciation of kindness, thankful.*

Think of a person in your life who you can describe as grateful. Explain why you believe this to be true. Are you willing to apply those same characteristics about yourself?

_____

_____

_____

_____

_____

_____

_____

_____

_____

_____

_____

_____

_____

_____

_____

_____

_____

_____

_____

Jennie Buelow

For Bella and Vivienne

*"It is in the quiet of your spirit and the hunger of your heart that prayer is born. He is always waiting, always listening, and always answers."*

CHAPTER 22

# Your Prayers

*Earnest*

Dear Daughter, have you ever prayed? If you have, what was the moment like? What brought you to the moment you felt a need to pour out your heart to God? To Jesus? What did you feel afterward?

I think prayer is a remarkable gem because what it evokes is intimacy. That intimacy is created when our hearts feel the need to empty its contents into the overflow that is God, and we search for Him to talk to Him. Praying is the beginning of you cultivating an intimate relationship with the Father. In your pursuit of that intimacy, prayer will be the most important thing you'll do. And the treasure you'll find in those moments will be an eventual yearning to do it often.

In fact, if you commit to praying at the start of each day, you'll learn the beauty of talking to the Father regularly. You'll find comfort and solace in His presence as you begin to realize

He is everywhere and He is always listening. That's one of the many things prayer does; it enables you to notice God in the details of your life. You see, an intentional, established prayer life places you in the presence of the Father, creating intimacy with Him so powerful that if you are going to be victorious, it is paramount. I know because transformation came for me at your age as I committed to delving deeper into my relationship with God through prayer. Actually, that's the only way it can happen.

Even though I recommend starting each day alone to talk with God, you can pray throughout your day. I pray everywhere: the grocery store, the bookstore, the gym, in my car driving. Everywhere. Because praying doesn't require us to be on our knees with our eyes closed and hands folded before us. But it does require us to talk to God. However, there should be times when you are alone with just your heart and God, speaking to Him and listening for what He will respond. That's when intimacy is born!

I was about your age watching my parents pray about everything our family experienced. Their prayers were rejoicing and triumphant in the good times, but they did the bended-knee, crying eyes, kind of praying when things weren't so good. My mother warred on her knees for my siblings' and my well-being, that our lives would always be cloaked in the overshadowing of the Holy Spirit, guided by the hand of God, and fashioned by the breath of Jesus.

But watching her didn't teach me how to pray, nor did listening to her pray teach me. What taught me to communicate with God about the details of my life was actually doing it myself. Sure, when my parents were being intentional gathering us all around the kitchen table to pray taught me that planning to pray regularly was the most important thing to bring me closer to my relationship with God. But then there came a point in my life where I wanted my own relationship with God, not be in the shadows of the relationship my mother had with God or the one my father had with Him. I wanted my own! So what they did do for me concerning prayer was teach me that without prayer it is impossible to have a relationship with Father God. When I watched them pray, the translation to me was that they wanted to be with Him and share the details of their lives with Him. It said they wanted to praise Him and give Him the respect and honor that is due a king, the King. It said they needed Him to cover the details of their lives and had faith that He would.

So I began talking to Him like I would talk to a friend. I didn't use fancy words or scream pleading platitudes. I simply talked to my Father about the details of my life. In so doing I often found myself worshipping—sometimes because my love for Him grew more and more each time as I learned more about Him and His love for me. And that is exactly what will happen for you as you design your own prayer life with God.

Who is your closest friend on earth? How much do you talk with this person? Is it every day? Several times a day? Do you spend time together daily? Weekly? Can you talk to him or her about anything and still feel safe and secure in your relationship with this person? Praying to the Father is much like talking to your friend. It is impossible to have a relationship with God and not pray or spend time alone with Him, much like a friend. It's best not to allow several days, weeks, or months to pass between the times you pray. Let's look at the importance of establishing a daily conversation with God. Praying.

We briefly talked above about how prayer creates an atmosphere of intimacy with God. Much like with anything else we want to grow, intimacy needs time and nurturing for it to grow as well. When we allow the lack of time to prevent us from communicating with the Father, intimacy is broken, and to re-establish it fosters feelings of starting over, which can further lead to the perception and feelings of reconnecting with God being insurmountable. This is exactly what the enemy wants to create. If he can get you to forego talking with God each day, he knows that getting you to fall short in your pursuit of righteousness will be easier because you've not talked to the Father first thing in the morning to cover the details of your day. First Peter 5:8 tells us to "be of sober spirit, be on the alert. Your adversary, the devil, prowls around like a roaring lion, seeking someone to devour." Praying or communicating or whatever you choose to label it is the biggest opportunity to ask God's help in challenging circumstances, to worship Him, to rest in Him, simply being quiet in His presence. But do it often.

"Rejoice always, pray without ceasing, in everything give thanks for this is the will of God in Christ Jesus for you" (1 Thessalonians 5:16–18).

Another reason you should pray every day is that the more you pray, the more you increase the opportunities to hear what God will say to you. I can't count the number of times in the middle of my prayer time, I have a thought, a Bible verse comes to my mind, or a line from a favorite worship song is the answer to what I had just been seeking clarity for! That's God speaking to me. Sure, it's a Bible verse that I've read hundreds of times, but God orchestrated the moment it became most real to me because He knew that moment would be the moment I would need it most. He will do the same thing for you when you've sung a song many times, but the time you need it most will be the time it pierces your heart and fills your mind and covers your circumstance. That's when you needed to hear from Him. That's how He is. That's what He does.

My younger daughter, Kerrigan, played elite soccer for US Girls Development Academy as a left forward. She's played soccer since she was five, but at nine years old, her journey as an elite player began. As a result, teams often invited her to guest play with their soccer clubs as a recruiting effort, as was the case when she played in the 2016 Las Vegas Mayor's Cup Soccer Tournament, Vegas Cup for short. As **one of the largest international youth soccer tournaments**, the Las Vegas Cup was created in 2000 by the city's mayor to further youth sports. It boasts of teams from around the world and about sixteen US states for girls and boys between the ages of eight to fifteen.

Kerrigan was enjoying a very successful tournament, performing well, and leading the team to a potential victory to win the entire tournament in the youth girls division. It was amazing watching her play with such passion and skill, outperforming her counterparts. But in the semifinal game, as Kerrigan was advancing the ball to score a goal, the goalie came out of the box to stop her shot, kneeing Kerrigan in the stomach. When Kerrigan went down, the gasps from the sideline spectators could be heard across the field. For me, her mom, the sound of her scream, coupled with having seen the collision, sent my heart into a tailspin! I remember praying to the Father to rush to her aid and overshadow her as she lay on the ground conscious but, from what we could see from the sideline, in pain. I asked God to enable her to stand and to infuse her body with his spirit so that she didn't sustain any injuries. Not so that she could go back into the game. I was more concerned with her not having suffered an injury and that she would be okay. Minutes later, she not only stood, but she walked to the sideline under everyone's applause. I was thrilled and thankful that Kerrigan was fine.

She planned not to go back into the game as she sat on the bench watching the game proceed without her. My husband and I were fine with that. Honestly, I was a bit relieved that she would not return to the game. But an unsettlement arose in me when, from time to time, my attention would divert from the field watching the game to Kerrigan sitting on the bench. I noticed she spoke to several of the other girls on the bench, even laughing at one point, having a fun-filled time sitting on the bench! They were not watching the game, cheering on their teammates on the field, but laughing and talking instead. I felt a bit unnerved, without peace. This team had invited her to help them win, and they were losing. I walked over to the bench where Kerrigan sat and asked her if she was hurt or injured because if she was injured, we needed to take her to the nearest emergency room. But if she was mildly hurt and didn't have any broken bones, then perhaps she could play through the hurt because sometimes that's what champions do. I had learned several years prior from Kierstin's soccer coach this was what he asked his players if they had been knocked around in a game.

So I told Kerrigan to discuss it with God and then feel confident with the decision she made. I wanted her to learn to finish what she started and not allow mishaps to divert her from participating in life. I wanted her to learn that sometimes life hurts us but that when we rely on God's direction, He renews us and causes us to triumph. That's what I wanted her prayer on the soccer sideline to be about. Asking God for His advice.

I went back to the parent sideline and prayed that God would reveal to Kerrigan what she needed to do. I prayed that He would speak to her in the moment as the game had restarted without her. I then began to thank Him for His wisdom in covering this situation. A few moments later, she was asking the coach to go back into the game. The left side of the soccer field is Kerrigan's comfort zone, being a left-footed striker. A midfielder sent the ball to her there, and she took no time shooting a long shot that sailed directly into the net as she scored the game-winning goal just before the clock ran out! We erupted in applause. Today, I don't know what prayer she prayed; I never asked. But I know she bowed her head on that soccer sideline and had a conversation with God.

What conversations do you need to have with Him? You may feel as though you don't know how to pray. You can pray anytime, anywhere, and about anything! If you know how to have an open, honest conversation with a friend, then you know how to pray because God is your friend and He hears everything you say. He is actually waiting for you to come to Him with your concerns and to spend time alone with Him. I must warn you, though. When you pray about a problem you need God to help you with or an answer for the problem, it may happen that you will wait and wait and wait some more to receive an answer. Moreover, that answer may come packaged in a completely different way than what you were expecting. The reason the answers to your prayers may not look like what you visualized or what you wanted is that God knows better than you can ever know what is best for you. He fashions your life the way you need it, not always the way you want it. Sometimes that fashioning God does to our lives hurts, but you can be assured that He hears every prayer and answers according to what is best for you.

Another vital part of establishing a relationship with God through praying is incorporating God's Word into your prayers. He loves it when you do that and is sure to respond to you telling Him what His promises are based on your requests. For example, let's say another person at your school or workplace has been harassing or bullying you, or a teacher or boss intimidates you by her stern demeanor. This bothers you because it's been happening for a long time, and it's making you afraid. Your prayer would be something like this:

*"God, I trust You as God of the universe, which is why I am praying to You—because You are almighty. You said in Your Word, the Bible, 'Have I not commanded you? Be strong and courageous! Do not be terrified or dismayed, for the Lord your God is with you wherever you go' (Joshua 1:9). Well, God, I am afraid. Please take away the power this person has over me and remind me that You are with me and You fight my battles. In Jesus' name. Amen."*

There is no way God ignores anything you say and doesn't answer your requests when you tell Him you are trusting His Word to be true. That is exactly what you are doing when you pray using scriptures. The only way you can tell God His promises to you through His Word is if you know His Word. What's the best way to know what God says? You must read your Bible!

Also, an effective prayer life incorporates thanksgiving. Daughter, always give thanks to God for everything. No matter how many problems you think you have or what is going wrong in your life, there is always something to be thankful for, as we learned about in a previous chapter. I love this verse so much, I am reiterating it here. Philippians 4:6 says, "Be anxious for nothing but in prayer and supplication with thanksgiving let your requests be known unto God." Giving thanks shows God you are grateful, which makes Him want to rush to your aid even more. Prayer is not complicated but simply a conversation with a friend. Your friend, God.

## Wearing Emeralds

Can you think of a challenge or problem you are enduring and you need God's help? In the space listed below, construct a prayer about your challenge. Be sure to find a Bible verse that reminds you that God promised to help you with this particular challenge.

_____

_____

_____

_____

_____

_____

_____

_____

_____

_____

_____

_____

_____

_____

_____

_____

_____

_____

_____

_____

_____

## Word Power

Earnest: *Resulting from or showing sincere and intense conviction.*

God loves when we are passionate about communicating with Him. Do you think sometimes, when you have a conversation with God, it requires you to be more passionate in your prayer than other times? Explain.

_____

_____

_____

_____

_____

_____

_____

_____

_____

_____

_____

_____

_____

_____

_____

Sharon Hambric
For Jordan

*"When money is earned honestly, a greater appreciation for it is born. I saw you love your earning power. God saw you love Him. I love you."*

CHAPTER 23

# Your Money

*Heir*

Money is the root of all evil! Have you heard that before? I've heard that statement so much in my life that sometimes it's on the tip of my tongue even now to regurgitate. People will recite it like a Bible verse pillaging the truth. The authentic version of this verse in the Bible that some have misinterpreted to fit their narrative is 1 Timothy 6:10, "For the love of money is the root of all evil and some by longing for it have wandered away from faith and pierced themselves with many griefs."

Daughter, money is *not* the root of all evil! Money is actually a gift from God. Deuteronomy 8:18, "But you shall remember the Lord your God, for it is He who is giving you power to make wealth, that he may confirm His covenant which He swore to your fathers, as it is this day." Moses is addressing the people of Israel, expounding deeply on how vitally important it is for them not to forget their God. He reminds them of the covenant made with their fathers and that their accumulation of wealth and their ability to get it are blessings and gifts from God.

Consider the word *love* in Deuteronomy 8:18 as you go back a few previous sentences. "For the love of money is the root of all evil." Why do you think Moses highlights and speaks quite extensively about the love of money? He never warned the Israelites against acquiring wealth, but he did stress a practice of giving immeasurable thanks for it. Moses knew that there were negative inclinations associated with prosperity and wealth. When an individual does not recognize God as having instilled the giftedness in them to attain wealth, they think they themselves are solely responsible for their financial success. When this is the case, Moses says pride is a dominant force in their characters and can lead to further abandonment of a relationship with God. His goal for the people of Israel was for them not to forget God as they began their journey out of the land of Egypt. Much like when we are beginning a new phase of our lives, it benefits us to remember that God is at the helm, and thankfulness should be at the core of what we do. Creating a healthy relationship with money is God's hope for each of us.

Given that, you are not too young to learn the value in managing the money you earn. At this point in your life, you may not be consistently earning money, but any amount of money you do earn should be managed well—allowances, babysitting, lifeguarding, tutoring, dog walking, etc. The biggest reason to begin with principles of managing your money at your age is that the more you learn about the biblical principles of money, paralleled with this youthful stage of your life, the more it sets you up for future monetary success.

According to the Bible, your parents are charged with teaching you about managing your money in God's way. They are your first line of defense to learn smart money moves. The best way your parents teach you is by modeling the behavior. As a teenager I learned many principles of managing money from my father, oftentimes listening to his advice or watching the standards he set for himself and our family. My father didn't believe in accumulating debt. One thing he always said when I was a teenager that resonates with me today is, "Outside of my house and my car, if I cannot pay cash for it, I must not need it." My father never used a credit card, never had debt, and retired ten years younger than retirement age.

So begin to take notice of the way your parents spend their money. What types of things do they spend their money on? What form of payment do they use to buy groceries and gasoline for their vehicles? Do they have credit cards? Ask your parents questions about their spending habits: the bills they pay, what a mortgage is, and how it relates to the type of home you live in. Finally, ask them what a budget is and what your family's budget looks like. All these questions relate to how well you manage the money you earn. Daughter, you are not too young to begin to manage your money the way God intends you to.

> "Train up a child the way he should go: and when he is old he will not depart from it."
>
> Proverbs 22:6

Now, I'm not going to sit here and tell you I listened to everything my father taught my siblings and me. I loved spending the money I earned from my first job in high school on the latest designer clothes, junk food, and entertainment. Every week I was spending money on something whether I needed it or not: theatre tickets, roller skating, music albums, the latest gadget. And do you know when my money ran out in any given week, I had the audacity to ask my parents for gas money to fill the car they bought me? Eventually I implemented smarter ways to manage the money I earned and brought those principles into my adult life. Many adults are making monetary mistakes late in life because they never learned principles for smart money management at your age.

Another large part of being successful at managing your money is directly related to the relationship you have with God. We're told throughout history that King Solomon was the wisest man who ever lived because he ruled based on the wisdom God dispensed to him. The Bible has a myriad of lessons to teach you about managing your money successfully. As with many other aspects of a life like yours—relationships with friends, extracurricular activities, academics—wisdom is required to make quality decisions about what God expects you to do with your money. How exactly does God expect you to manage your money? The Bible explicitly and very frequently explains three principles Christians are to use to be in complete obedience to God's Word concerning money.

I've learned the basis of good financial practice and monetary responsibility, God's way, is based largely on three things to execute: give, save, and spend, in that order.

## 1. Give

During the exodus of the Israelites from Egypt, the Israelites were charged with giving ten percent of what they earned from the production of their crops to the administrators and leaders who led the exodus because they had no crops or animals to till the land. Much like they gave, we are to give to our churches and pay our taxes to the government we live under so that it can continue to function. It was the law in biblical times and giving to our churches and paying taxes to our government is the law today. Think about what would happen if we did not give to our churches and our government. The churches would have to close their doors, and the government would shut down, and we as a nation would no longer be protected. Malachi 3:10 instructs us to "bring the whole tithe into the storehouse, so there may be food in my house and prove me now herewith, saith the LORD of hosts, if I will not open you the, if I will not open for you the windows of heaven and pour you out a blessing until it overflows." In the Bible the word *tithe* means ten percent of annual produce or earnings taken as a tax for church and the clergy. The church serves the surrounding communities and desperately depends on its members to unite in positioning the church to provide the needs of the community. Daughter, you can actually give anything you have. The more you give, the more God will honor you in your need. No, your provision for your need is not dependent on whether you give because God will always supply your need, always. However, when your heart is open to giving, you will see unspeakable things being given to you! Again, my father taught my siblings and me this, but I regret it being much later in my adult life I began to practice giving.

Giving is not solely tied to our tithing; give whatever you have. You can give of your time, volunteering at various needy shelters, schools, churches. You can donate things you no longer use to people who can use them. Any of your resources can be given to someone who can benefit from them. When we foster giving hearts, we have a sense of contentment and peace that becomes a part of our character, and we never need to worry about our own needs being met.

A few years ago, my husband wrecked his car in an accident about five miles from our home. A high school student ran a stop sign directly hitting his car at a high impact. The impact was so great that it totaled my husband's car. Before the accident, we had planned to keep that car for a long time because it held its value and was a classic in its class by industry standards. Thankfully, both my husband and the student walked away from the accident unscathed. But reality set in to the fact that we would need to purchase not one new vehicle but two. One to replace my husband's car and one for our then ninth-grader Kierstin, who was eagerly anticipating having her first car to drive herself around town. The problem was we had only budgeted for one car, not two, and I didn't want to interrupt our family savings. I knew that we had been obedient to God's Word in giving of our resources and tithes, but worry still sat on my heart. Then, as I was praying, a thought came to my remembrance. About ten years prior to this time in our lives when Martin and I had purchased new vehicles for ourselves. We decided to keep our old vehicles instead of trading them because they were in such good condition. Shortly after, we gave those vehicles to friends who we later found out needed vehicles because theirs had stopped functioning properly. Bringing that fact to my mind in a moment I was desperate for God to intervene was like Him saying directly to me, "Don't you remember the two cars you and Martin gave away to your friends? What kind of God would I be if I don't give you what you need now?" I felt such a sweet peace come over me and never worried about it again.

As I was walking downstairs, my husband called. He was thrilled! He had been sharing with a friend our situation of needing to purchase two new vehicles. The providence of God had positioned my husband to be sharing his heart with a friend who had a friend who owned a car dealership and promised to give him a good deal. And that he did, not for one but for two new vehicles! By giving away two vehicles to friends ten years prior, we were unknowingly planting seeds for a future need we would have. Give.

## 2. Save

I Never—yes, never with a capital N for emphasis—saved money as a teenager. *Why would I do that?* I often thought when my dad was suggesting I do. I had worked really hard at my first job to earn my own money, and I wanted to spend it, not save it. Spending was more fun for me than saving. Girl, do not adopt that position!

When Egypt was to experience the great famine, God sent Joseph to tell Pharaoh to set aside resources in preparation. Read in Genesis 41:34–36 about how Pharaoh saved twenty percent of the harvested grain during the seven good years to prepare for the seven bad years that were coming. That's called saving! Saving is you planning to succeed. When you save, you are preparing for your future, your short-term future, and your long-term future. You're also planning for unforeseen events in your life that can cause you to need financial resources that you may not otherwise have. The amount of money you save depends largely on the amount of money you earn. These are more good questions to ask your parents: what their savings plans for their futures look like and what the savings plan for the family looks like.

## 3. Spending

Spending is fun, isn't it? Especially when we are the subject of whom the spending is for. The heavenly Father wants you to enjoy the fruit of your labor. That means you work hard for the money you earn, so God wants you to enjoy spending it, but wisely. Spending wisely means spending after you've given and after you've saved. Spend seventy percent. It means spending to pay your bills to avoid debt. It also means spending on things that will add value to your life. The apostle Paul in 1 Thessalonians 4:11–12 says this, "Make it your ambition to lead a quiet life and attend to your own business and work with your hands, just as we commanded you, so that you will behave properly toward outsiders and not be in any need." Paul is simply saying to spend your earnings on lifestyle choices that are commensurate with what is earned and not try to impress other people. Spend in a way that you avoid needing to depend on other people.

Daughter, God's plan for you concerning money is that you use your gifts and talents to earn it and that you manage it well.

Managing your money well includes giving, saving, and spending. Using this three-tiered approach to managing your money as a guide sets you up for success and enables you to avoid financial bondage. I'd like to reiterate you are not too young to learn sound financial practices to enrich your life. The sooner you learn these practices, the longer you have to benefit from them. Are you ready to show God that you can be a good steward of the money He blesses you with?

## Wearing Emeralds

Write a list of questions below that you would like to discuss with your parents about how they manage their money. Remember to incorporate into your questions the family budget, savings plans, investments they have, and the type of bills they pay.

_____

_____

_____

_____

_____

_____

_____

_____

_____

_____

_____

_____

_____

_____

_____

_____

_____

_____

_____

## Word Power

Heir: *A person inheriting and continuing the legacy of a predecessor.*

Write about what you think it means to be God's heir. What does that mean for your life and relationship with Jesus, God's Son?

_____

_____

_____

_____

_____

_____

_____

_____

_____

_____

_____

_____

_____

_____

_____

_____

_____

_____

_____

Brandi Johnson

For Jourdan, Sanaa, Syrai

*"You are everything God told me you would be when I carried you. In life, everything good and everything difficult is His will and you will be okay. Remember his presence in your life is greater than the presence of the enemy."'*

## CHAPTER 24

# Your Spiritual Gifts

*Amazing*

Dear Daughter, when a person becomes a Christian, their purpose in life is to contribute to building God's kingdom; in other words, sharing who God is with people who don't know Him. Fulfilling your purpose in life looks different for everyone, but ultimately the goal is the same. For one person it could mean counseling the brokenhearted or starting a ministry to help homeless people; for another it could mean teaching the Word of God. Whatever your purpose is, God equips you with spiritual gifts to be successful in fulfilling your purpose. What is a spiritual gift? Spiritual gifts are endowments that are given to Christians by the Holy Spirit to empower us to help and to serve others. Spiritual gifts are unlike gifts and talents in that spiritual gifts become alive and are illumined once you become a Christian because it is then the Holy Spirit becomes alive in you, and the Holy Spirit is the dispenser of spiritual gifts. Spiritual gifts build the body of Christ, which means to support and aid those who have declared Jesus as their Lord and Savior. While it may take a moment for you to fully understand and grasp the concept of spiritual gifts, it is clearly defined several times throughout the Bible. In 1 Peter, the apostle expounds on this point, and we get a greater understanding of how we are to use the spiritual gifts God has given to each of us. "As each one has received a special gift, employ it in serving one another, as good stewards of the manifold grace of God" (1 Peter 4:10).

> "But to each one is given the manifestation of the Spirit for the common good."
>
> 1 Corinthians 12:7

Spiritual gifts are not to be confused with talents or giftedness, which was written about several chapters ago. A person may have the ability to sing well, paint, run fast, or design clothes; those are all talents a person may have and can be used to serve others. But spiritual gifts are in addition to your talents and giftedness if a person is a Christian. They are solely for the purpose of helping others to come into their relationship with the Father and function to aid others once they do. People who don't believe in God may only have talents and possess giftedness in a certain area. But they don't have spiritual gifts because spiritual gifts are given by the Holy Spirit. Whether you are a Christian or not, don't feel pressured or uncomfortable by the knowledge of spiritual gifts.

When my husband and I first joined the church we currently attend, as part of the membership process, we were required to complete a spiritual gifts assessment test to determine which area of ministry we would be volunteers in. When our daughters became older, they were given the spiritual gifts assessment test as well. The test consisted of a myriad of questions, statements, traits, and beliefs that the individual taking the assessment rates according to how he or she feels the statements are true about themselves. At the completion of the test, a score is given. The test is not a pass or fail but is simply used as a guide to use personally in self-actualization. It benefitted me tremendously to learn about myself and those things in my personality that I was innately endowed with to help others learn about their own relationship with God. That is the purpose of spiritual gifts.

I encourage you to take a spiritual gifts test. Just for fun. You can easily find one on a Google search on the internet. Once you complete the test, determine what it states your spiritual gifts are. Study it and ask yourself questions. Do you agree with the results? Is there evidence in your life to validate or invalidate its findings? What happens next if you agree with the results? How do you move forward? All these are good questions that help you to become introspective to learn more about your current self to empower your future self.

Let's take a look at some of the spiritual gifts the Bible mentions: prophecy, teaching, encouraging, giving, leadership, mercy, wisdom, knowledge, faith, helps.

Prophecy is described as the ability to speak to an individual about future events in their lives to disclose the purposes of God for their lives in any given situation. Often God has revealed to this individual the direction and path one must take regarding their life. The revelation can come in many different ways, which include through reading the Bible, having a conversation, or a feeling one has.

Teaching is exactly as the name implies but with respect to spiritual gifts, explaining and exposing the Word of God into an individual's life. Oftentimes you recognize this gift on a Sunday morning when you attend church. The pastor is teaching you the ways of God. Or it could look like a Wednesday night women's Bible study.

Encouraging is used to build others up to strengthen their faith. Being empathetic as you support emotionally the trials of another's life. Perhaps you are constantly encouraging your friends and family members as they face trials of life.

Giving is when an individual is genuinely concerned about the needs of others and enthusiastically provides the need, whether that need is financial, material, time, or attention. I love giving my resources, time, and talents to people. The look of joy and peace that dons their faces after I've given something to them fuels me to give more and more of myself.

Leadership directs, guides, and manages others in the church. People possessing this gift are easily recognizable as well because they are in the midst of others instructing and orchestrating things for a larger framework of a company or business.

Mercy shows sympathy and compassion to others while they are in negative circumstances of life. The person with mercy's character is open and inviting.

Word of wisdom is the gift of someone who can understand the biblical truths and speak them in life situations at apropos moments.

Word of knowledge is, like wisdom, a speaking gift ascribed to someone who can understand the biblical truths and the deep things of God.

Faith is given to all believers of God. However, the spiritual gift of faith is exhibited in the person who is unwavering in her thinking despite outside circumstances. Her faith is so unshakeable that she exudes confidence in God's ability to affect situations through her prayers.

Helps is the spiritual gift that enables an individual to assist and aid the body of the church in circumstances of their lives. This person is kindhearted, compassionate, and empathetic, always offering herself to serve others in some capacity.

The Bible speaks of many other spiritual gifts in various parts of the Bible. Here is a list of places you can go to further study spiritual gifts:

- Romans 12:6–8
- 1 Corinthians 12:4–11
- 1 Corinthians 12:28

Daughter, remember you cannot pick a spiritual gift and decide, "That's the one I want!" You already possess it. As you grow in your relationship with God, it will naturally grow in your character and personality. You will begin to recognize in yourself and others some of the spiritual gifts listed above and others listed in the Bible. Many times, I have called a friend with a problem I was facing, and after she listened intently she would inevitably reply, not with advice on what to do but with words of encouragement or wisdom from God's Word or knowledge of what she could see the outcome to be based on what I had told her. Her spiritual gifts are sure, and I love talking to and fellowshipping with her! She, indeed, is using her gifts to build my faith in my relationship with God. That's what spiritual gifts are designed to do: to strengthen the faith of those around us. Spiritual gifts are always used to help or strengthen another person or group of people. Always!

Think back to similar situations in your own life and determine whether you can pinpoint the spiritual gifts in some of your friends, parents, siblings, and teachers. What about in yourself?

Do you love to see a person's face light up when you give something they were not expecting? Do you offer words of encouragement to those you come in contact with whose hearts are sad and broken? Do you like to teach others things about God that you've learned? Your spiritual gifts are mighty for serving others and being obedient to God. You naturally enjoy carrying out the act of your spiritual gift without realizing it. It's in your character. And the sweetest thing about your spiritual gift is that you can never lose it!

## Wearing Emeralds

Think of all the people—friends, siblings, parents, teachers—you come in contact with on a regular basis. Pick one of those people to identify a spiritual gift in their character. It does not have to be one listed in the text but can also be one that the person repeatedly exudes; it's a part of their personality. Now take a moment to describe why you think this person has the spiritual gift you have listed.

_____

_____

_____

_____

_____

_____

_____

_____

_____

_____

_____

_____

_____

_____

_____

_____

_____

## Word Power

Amazing: *Causing great surprise or wonder, astonishing, startlingly impressive.*

Did you know before now that you impress the Father? Describe things about yourself or life that you think would impress God.

_____

_____

_____

_____

_____

_____

_____

_____

_____

_____

_____

_____

_____

_____

_____

_____

_____

_____

_____

_____

Kylee Washington
For Eboni

*"Marry the man who loves Jesus more than he loves you. For a man who loves and is loved by Jesus will love you the way He loves His bride...sacrificially, devotedly, and faithfully forever."*

## CHAPTER 25

# Your Dating

*Lovely*

Dear Daughter, dating is a very important part of growing into the young lady God has destined you to be. For many of you reading this book, dating is not in your immediate future because you may be too young to date, but it is still a good idea to learn about dating habits so that when it is time for you to date, you have planned things out. It's always best to plan ahead how you will carry out an action before you are met with having to decide in the moment. Others of you reading this book have probably been dating for quite some time. You, too, can always learn new things to put into practice as you're meeting potential date mates.

Do you know that God created courtship and dating especially for you? He is such an attentive God, and He wants to give you everything you need and your heart's desire. He knew at some point in your development you would develop the desire to date, to desire friendship and companionship of the opposite sex that culminates in romance and marriage. His love for you is so amazing, sometimes indescribable, and complete that it covers every aspect of your life. He is love and wants you to experience His love, which sometimes comes through other people. I know when we think of God, we don't think of Him creating romance for us to enjoy. But biblical scholars believe the Song of Solomon in the Bible, all eight chapters, is a song and an actual love letter. It's filled with such poetic imagery to depict reality as Solomon recounts his very own courtship of his future bride with romantic thoughtfulness. "How beautiful you are my darling; How beautiful you are! Your eyes are like doves behind your veil, your hair is like a flock of goats that have ascended from Mount Gilead" (Song of Solomon 4:1). Another reads, "To me my darling, you are like my mare among the chariots of Pharaoh. Your cheeks are lovely with ornaments, your neck with strings of beads" (Song of Solomon 1:9–10). Quite romantic, yes?

You should take some time to read the Song of Solomon to note the countless expressions of love and how romantic they are as Solomon prepares to take the Shulammite girl as his bride. It holds in high esteem the purity of marital affection and romance.

While the world may view dating and courtship as a very casual act of engaging as many people as you possibly can to "find the right one," God's standard for your dating and courtship habits are quite different. He clearly uses Paul's instructions to the Corinthians to instruct you on forming friendships and courtships.

"Do not be bound together with unbelievers; for what partnership have righteousness and lawlessness, or what fellowship has light with darkness?"

2 Corinthians 6:14

When you begin to date, you are dating with the purpose of aligning yourself with another person who shares your love of Jesus Christ, a potential life partner. When you enter into a courtship with someone who also loves God and declares Jesus Christ as the center of his life, God grows that love, and you can celebrate it as a gift God Himself has given you. You can trust it, rely on it, and feel comfort in this love God bestows upon you.

When you choose to date someone who does not share your love of God or recognize that Jesus is the Son of the one true God, you will experience discord in that relationship because God is not at the center. You will easily, perhaps, recognize when God is not at the center of a relationship because the relationship will not bear the characteristics of love. My friend Lisa and I discuss this often, as we both have two daughters.

Love is patient, love is kind, it is not jealous; love does not brag, it is not arrogant. It does not act disgracefully, it does not seek its own benefit; it is not provoked, does not keep an account of a wrong suffered, it does not rejoice in unrighteousness, but rejoices with the truth; it keeps every confidence, it believes all things, hopes all things, endures all things. Love never fails.

1 Corinthians 13:4–8

Daughter, you will easily be able to recognize God in the person you have chosen to date because God is love, and love looks just like God.

When I was seventeen, I was dating a young man my parents weren't sure was a good match for my character. I remember my mother telling me she sensed that he was not fully engaged in getting to know who I was. At the time, I didn't understand how she could come to that realization. As our relationship grew into months of dating, I began to understand exactly what my mother sensed. This young man became comfortable starting arguments with me about almost anything. He criticized my choices and belittled my thoughts. It became clear to me he was not someone I wanted to continue to spend time with as the relationship became a burden to me. Instead of enjoying his company, I began to dread seeing him. The space between him and me was no longer a place where God's love could take root and grow. I learned from that experience the wisdom to recognize when someone was not good for me and the courage to remove him from my life. He was the first and last young man I brought home to meet my parents until I met my husband. I learned anyone who did not honor his relationship with God was not worthy of me nor worthy of meeting my family. Taking that stance saved me so much time and heartache. And it protected my virtue. You should never give anyone access to you who doesn't desire access to Jesus.

There are three important keys to dating every young girl your age should know, and you should ask yourself three important questions before you begin to date.

1. Protect your journey to discover who you are and ask yourself, "Will dating interrupt my journey to discover who I am?"

   At your age it's impossible to know completely who you are. You are so young; you are continually evolving as a person as you navigate life. You are discovering your likes and dislikes, what interests you, who interests you. You are being introduced to new things, embracing some and discarding others. So to completely know who you are at this age is impossible. But! You do have an idea of what you stand for and what interests you. These things are all part of the journey you are on for self-discovery. And this is important because as you begin to date, you want to choose people whose own values align with yours. People who will enhance your journey, not detract from it.

2. Know your purpose for dating at this time in your life and ask yourself, "Why do I want to date now?"

   If you have not yet begun to date, that means your parents have decided you may be too young. But when you are old enough to date, your dating should begin with a healthy discussion between you and your parents about what is a good age for you to begin dating. In the same discussion, your parents should set boundaries for your dating so that all parties—you, your parents, and the young man—are clear on what expectations are set for your dating habits. This way the lines of communication are drawn and open. Relay to the person you're dating the boundaries that you and your parents have set for you. Things like where you are allowed to go, if there will be adult supervision, what time you will be returning home, if your date will be allowed to come to your home, if you will be allowed to spend time at your date's home, what types of things you will be doing together, if your date drives and you are allowed in your date's car. You see, there are so many different facets to dating that it is definitely something you want to discuss with your parents firsthand. I'm not advocating meeting a young man, taking him home to your parents, and them telling him, "These are the rules my parents have set for me to date you." But I am saying it is your responsibility as a young lady to show the person you have chosen to date what those expectations are simply by your actions and conversations you engage with him. You can set the tone and pace of a dating relationship. If you've already been dating for some time now, self-reflect and use these keys to move forward.

3. Decide before you begin that you will date only individuals worthy of your time. Ask yourself, "What makes someone worthy to date me?"

The answer? Someone whose values parallel yours.

Typically, I've found that young girls between the ages of thirteen and fifteen want to begin dating to open their circle of friends, to meet new people, to share companionship. Not at all in pursuit of romance. Though, when your body is changing as you are entering puberty and you're desiring to explore how to process those feelings that come with puberty, one of the main feelings is romantic attraction to the opposite sex. This is a natural progression of your body and mind, and those feelings should be embraced, as they mean you have the capacity to express love within the confines of age appropriateness and what the Word of God says about doing so.

When you think you are ready to date, desiring to share your time, ideas, and interests with a boy as he shares those same things with you for the purpose of sharing a bond where God is the center and is glorified, you can often date young men who have already been a part of your circle of friends. This is when it is time to initiate the conversation with your parents.

But! What happens when you think you are ready to date and your parents disagree?

Daughter, approach the conversation with your parents very humbly and openly, deciding beforehand that the purpose of the conversation is not to change their minds but to express your thoughts and to gain an understanding of theirs. In the end, your position is to be completely obedient to your parent's decision, and that show of maturity could be the gem that changes their minds if you think you are ready to begin dating.

I pray your dating experience is clothed by the presence of the Holy Spirit and that the young man you date sees you the way the Father sees you: beautifully, wonderfully, and empowered!

## Wearing Emeralds

Use the space below to list the reasons why you think you are ready to date. How will you approach the subject with your parents?

If you are old enough to date, use the space below to list positive things about yourself that you are excited for others to get to know.

_____

_____

_____

_____

_____

_____

_____

_____

_____

_____

_____

_____

_____

_____

_____

_____

_____

## Word Power

Lovely: *Exquisitely beautiful.*

Love is the character of God. Who in your life do you have a deep love for? Describe the relationship.

_____

_____

_____

_____

_____

_____

_____

_____

_____

_____

_____

_____

_____

_____

_____

_____

_____

_____

_____

_____

_____

_____

Shondreka Helire
For Cadence and Caylee

*"Sometimes in life on the journey to discover yourself and shape your character, life will make you feel small. But the impact of how big you truly are rests in the honesty of your word."*

## CHAPTER 26

# Your Word

*Integrous*

Dear Daughter, do you know that God has never broken a promise, gone against anything He has ever said, or not done what He said He would? Never! If you search the world over, even in the most remote parts, search the most highly esteemed academic community, search for the most religious and faithful pedagogue or expositor of God's Word, you will not find one whose word is always right and dependable and whose character is unmatched. His Word is always true. The knowledge of that should comfort you in ways that illumine and enhance your perspective of Him and elevate your relationship with Him. It's truly remarkable when you really think about what that means. It means you can always trust Him to always do what He says He will, no matter what! When you understand that God cannot break His word to you, then you will find the same comfort, and your relationship with Him will not only grow but will be a place of solace for you. Being able to trust our God, who captivates our hearts so profoundly, brings a peace so all-consuming, it's practically unbelievable until you experience it yourself. That's what He wants: you to experience Him fully in ways you can't imagine.

Think about all your friends and acquaintances. When I think about mine, I think how easy it is to be in a relationship with those whose word I know I can count on to be true and honest. Those with whom I don't feel the same level of comfort, it's uncomfortable for me to engage. So I rarely do, and when I do, my expectations are not high. No one should accept anyone feeling that their word is not dependable and they can't be relied upon in a friendship, the workplace, or organizations.

Remember we discussed how a part of identity is built on several character traits, and those traits, in concert, are a large part of creating who you are. One of those traits is trust. When we really look at the concept of trust, the benefit of its power frames everything we do because trust or the lack of trust is the foundation of our success in anything: relationships, work, pursuits, and everything you do. Trust is at the basis of you giving your word. Here's what happens when there is a lack of trust:

1. Your word becomes worthless. When a person's word is no longer of value, respect is lost, and that can be a lonely place to be when no one respects you.
2. Trust is difficult to regain. It can be done, but the road to regaining it is one that has to intentionally be walked. You must first admit to yourself that you have broken

trust of others and ask yourself why, have the difficult conversation that you are committed to correcting your mistake, and then practice keeping your word.

3.  You could become isolated. When a person repeatedly lies and breaks promises and commitments, news of it spreads like wildfire out of control.

4.  Your reputation suffers. A person's reputation is evaluated in business and in personal relationships as well.

When an individual is able to be trusted, being in a relationship with him or her, whether personal or business-related, is priceless. It is comforting because you know without doubt he or she will always be reliable and trusted to follow through on their word given to you.

Giving your word, making a promise to someone, and whether you follow through is one thing that contributes not only to defining your character but also how successful your relationship with other people will be. When someone continuously breaks their word, they can be seen as a liar.

> By this we know that we have come to know Him, if we keep His commandments. The one who says, "I have come to know Him," and does not keep His commandments, is a liar, and the truth is not in him; but whoever keeps His word, in him the love of God has truly been perfected.
>
> 1 John 2:3–5

Think about it. Do you ever again trust a person who has continually shown you they are lying? Forgiving someone for lying and being able to trust them again is different. For the person who has continuously lied, it is indeed a character flaw, and their identity suffers dearly.

Keeping your word says integrity is important to you and you want others to know that you are a person of worth, you can be trusted, and you value relationships where truth and honesty reign supreme. In essence, your word becomes a reflection of your character. When you make a practice of keeping your word, then you're building a part of your character that is positive and truthful. When you continually break your word and promises to others, you are destroying the foundation of your character and filling that foundation with such a negative trait that it could actually affect other parts of your life. Here's an example: What if you told a friend on three different occasions you would meet her in the library after school to help her prepare for a Spanish test she would be taking in a week? Each time she waited and waited for you to no avail. You never showed up because there was always something more important you needed to do. Your friend finally decided to stop trusting you, but you didn't know because you really didn't see the problem with not showing up. Each time you called her the same evening to apologize. Then one day you needed your friend to write a letter of recommendation for a new tutoring job at the library where compensation for your services would benefit you monetarily. She told you that she couldn't write the letter because she was not confident that you would be on time each time you needed to tutor someone. You were flabbergasted to learn that your friend no longer trusted you to do what you said you would do. In your friend's eyes, you disregarded her time and needs on more occasions than one and then expected her to write you a letter of recommendation for a job you couldn't follow through on with her! Here's what she probably thinks you are: irresponsible, untruthful, selfish, and rude. The foundation of your character is breaking!

God certainly doesn't expect you to be perfect; that's impossible. What God does expect from you is that you know the standard by which you are to live and commit to trying your best to live by it. The standard is His word relayed to us through the Bible. God will never lie to you, nor will He break His word to you. Our hearts' desire should be to mirror His character.

The Bible is filled with examples of people not committing to doing what they said they would do and the negative effects it brought into other people's lives as well as their own. The most pressing example of a person breaking his word was that of the apostle Peter. When Jesus' crucifixion was nearing the fulfillment of time, He was talking to His disciples about what was going to happen. And he said, "I say to you Peter, the rooster will not crow today until you have denied three times that you know Me" (Luke 22:34, NASB). It saddened Peter to learn that Jesus believed he would deny ever knowing Him. He loved Jesus; they were friends and had enjoyed a friendship committed to teaching others. So Peter said to Jesus, "Even if I have to die with You, I will not deny You." All the disciples said the same thing too (Matthew 26:35, NASB). Not long after, Peter denied knowing Jesus three times, not once but three times, just as Jesus had told him he would. Peter had become afraid of being associated with Jesus, fearful for his own life. The crucifixion certainly did not hinge on Peter's word, and although he did not cause Jesus' crucifixion, Peter told Jesus he would die with Him before he denied knowing Him. I don't think Peter was lying. I think he was very heartfelt when he said he would support Jesus. But fear consumed him, and in a moment of desperation, he did exactly what Jesus said he would. He denied knowing Jesus when taunted by Jesus' enemies. When Peter was faced with death himself, he did not have the courage to stand firm in the words he said to Jesus. I'd like to think, outside of a death threat, that when you are under pressure to stand firm in a previous word you've given, you will. Peter actually became ashamed of his actions, and he appeared as a liar to those who had actually seen him with Jesus. Do you think Peter's character suffered as a result? Yes, it did!

Daughter, it is hard to regain the trust of an individual whom you have given your word to and then broken your word. God's Word instructs us very vividly against breaking our word.

> Then Moses spoke to the heads of the tribes of the sons of Israel, saying, "This is the word which the Lord has commanded. If a man makes a vow to the Lord, or takes an oath to bind himself with a binding obligation, he shall not violate his word; he shall do according to all that proceeds out of his mouth."
>
> Numbers 30:1–2

Have you ever had someone tell you they were going to do something that involved you, and then they didn't do it? Or maybe they said they wouldn't do something that could bring harm to you, and they actually did? How did that make you feel?

You probably felt a gamut of different emotions, one of which was committing to not trusting a word that person speaks! Remember your actions speak louder than your words, and your words can quickly devalue who God intended you to be.

What about keeping your word to yourself? Keeping your word to yourself is equally as important as keeping your word to others, if not more important. Keeping your word to yourself indicates a mature you, able to set goals and follow through on them. When you keep your word to yourself through setting goals and accomplishing those goals, you learn to trust yourself and, therefore, establish a foundation of trust in your relationships with other people.

## Wearing Emeralds

Can you think of a time you broke your word to a friend? Or a time she broke her word to you? How did either time make you feel? Make two columns. In the first column, make a list of single words to describe how you felt after breaking your word to a friend. In the second column, make a list of single words to describe how you felt after a friend broke her word to you. Compare the lists.

| When I broke my word, I felt: | When she broke her word, I felt: |
|---|---|
| | |
| | |
| | |
| | |
| | |
| | |
| | |

## Word Power

Integrous: *Having or characterized by integrity.*

Explain, according to the chapter, the main reason why keeping your integrity intact is important.

---

Stephanie Webb

For McKenzie and Autumn

*"You are more than enough. This world needs everything about you, and no amount of disappointment, challenge, or difficulty can change that. Lead with kindness, give generously, and know that God and I love you endlessly. With God not you nor your virtue can fail."*

# CHAPTER 27

# Your Virtue

*Virtuous*

Dear Daughter, the meaning of virtue is quite varied and cannot singularly pinpoint one trait, but at the root of its variations, it is the same basic concept: that of a character that inevitably leads to a behavior worthy of praise. Virtue is not a trait that is donned at an opportunistic moment, nor is it that which is discarded if you suddenly aren't feeling the "outfit" anymore. Rather virtue is a state of mind, a state of being, a state of a high moral standard. You can't arrive at virtue. It's a process along the road to identity where you gather gems along the way.

When I was growing up, as I have mentioned, my father was the officiating pastor of the church he started. From a little girl I watched him become this huge status of a man in character whom the entire congregation had such admiration and adoration for. He was kind, thoughtful, and giving of his time and resources to the members of his church as well as the surrounding community. My mother was the same way. The phone calls she took in the middle of the night. The meals she cooked for an ill congregant. The hospital visits they took together to pray for people. They became known as honest, dependable, giving, and kind people across the state we lived in. At home it was a little different. Just a little. My parents showed triple kindness, thoughtfulness, honesty, and dependability to me and my siblings. Initially when I thought back on those moments in time, I wasn't sure how they managed to be so steadfast in serving their church, community, and our home. But their goodness rang out loud and clear as echoes of their virtue resonate even today.

It just seemed so easy for them. But I'm sure it wasn't. But where did they learn those character traits culminating in their virtue? From their parents?

As Christians, actually, as humans, we are charged with the task of striving for virtue. Unfortunately, the world we live in today rarely applauds or values virtuous behavior. But remember as a beautiful child of the one true God, you don't live by the world's standards but by God's.

The Bible, your roadmap for righteousness, is saturated with sweet instructional notes about virtue. Paul writes to the Philippians:

> "Finally, brethren, whatever is true, whatever is honorable, whatever is right, whatever is pure, whatever is lovely, whatever is of good repute, if there is any excellence and if anything, worthy of praise, dwell on these things."
>
> Philippians 4:8

It's actually through living a righteous life bathed in God's hue that you are virtuous. As you grow in your relationship with God, you become more virtuous because, in essence, you are mirroring His character. Oh! To be like Him, in His image, we can only imagine! Girl, your virtue is for all to see on a daily basis. You may be looking at all the words in the Bible verse above that merge to define a virtuous character. You may be thinking how you will live up to all those wonderfully descriptive words and whether anyone will ever use them to describe you. Those words describe you because Christ lives in you, and He is all these things and more.

Remember virtue is not something you put on and then take off like your favorite pair of jeans. It's a way of thinking, a mindset. Once your mind is open to embracing one characteristic of virtue, it further expands to embrace another, then another, and another until your moral excellence shines. Look over the characteristics of virtue again, revisiting Philippians 4:8. How is it possible to live by things that are true and not be honest? Can you champion things that are just and do not operate in purity? When have you ever thought on things that are good and not described them as lovely? You see, when the things that describe a person's virtue or the characteristics of virtue are interrelated, those characteristics become an individual's character. That's what virtue inside of your hearts and minds does. It takes a firm root on the foundation of your heart and divides it into many different parts to serve you.

In 2005 my nephews came to live with our family as a result of having been displaced by Hurricane Katrina. They were very sad, shy, and withdrawn because they didn't know when they would be able to return to their homes and schools. Their lives were filled with uncertainty. But my girls were very kind and generous. My girls' hearts were so sweet, and their smiles were broad. I saw their love when they took turns standing at the front door watching guard for the boys' arrival. Their kindness blossomed each time they offered the boys whatever they needed. Kierstin and Kerrigan showed respect for the boys when they wouldn't enter the space we together created for them unless the boys invited them. Not once did my girls relay to them that they were outsiders living in our house. Kierstin and Kerrigan's virtue shone through like the sun rising across the horizon to set the stage for a gloriously beautiful day! I remember being so proud of them!

Here's what the message Bible says in Philippians 4:8–9 (MSG):

> Summing it all up, friends, I'd say you'll do best by filling your minds and meditating on things true, noble, reputable, authentic, compelling, gracious— the best, not the worst; the beautiful, not the ugly; things to praise, not things to curse. Put into practice what you learned from me, what you heard and saw and realized. Do that, and God who makes everything work together, will work you into his most excellent harmonies.

Oh, the beauty in being virtuous! Christian Daughters, strive for it, and you will find it growing inside of you like wildflowers! Wildflowers are beautiful! Let truth be your compass, protect your reputation, come alive in your authenticity, feel compelled, show graciousness (the kind Jesus shows you each time you fall), see the best in people and circumstances (not the worst), look for the beautiful in others (not the ugly), give praise with your words (not curses). Do all these things and feel your virtue rising up! Others will want to be around you, and when you recognize virtue in others, you'll want to be in their presence as well. But don't keep it to yourself. God calls us to go out into the world to show others himself in us. Are you ready?

## Wearing Emeralds

Revisit the two versions of Philippians 4:8: The Message and the New American Standard Bible. Extract from those verses the words that describe virtue. Then use the two columns below—one labeled "I have these" and the other labeled "I want these"—to list your words. Here's an example.

| I have these | I want these |
| --- | --- |
|  |  |
|  |  |
|  |  |
|  |  |
|  |  |
|  |  |
|  |  |

## Word Power

Virtuous: *Having or showing high moral standards.*

What are some examples of having high moral standards? Who is the first person you think of described as so?

_____

_____

_____

_____

_____

_____

_____

_____

_____

_____

_____

_____

_____

_____

_____

_____

_____

_____

_____

_____

Connie Vasey
For Crystal

*"Every time you make the right choice, those rooted in righteous-*
*ness, it won't always be the popular choice. Have the courage to*
*do so anyway. Every moment is an opportunity to live above and*
*beyond the world's expectations of you. When you choose righ-*
*teousness, this sets you on a path of spiritual growth and fulfills*
*my desire that you make a difference in the earth."*

CHAPTER 28

# Your Choices

*Wise*

Dear Daughter, to have the ability to choose is a beautiful and wonderful gift from God. He is the Creator of the universe, and His creations are perfect! Do you know He could have created you, everyone, without the ability to choose? Imagine not being able to choose your friends, your clothes, what you eat, where you go, the car you drive, where you vacation, when you go to sleep, when you wake up. Imagine what your life would be like then. Imagine. Bondage, not freedom. But! Our amazing God loved you so much that He created you with choice, the power to choose! I shudder just thinking of the love in that.

The choices you make have extraordinary power and last-ing effects on your life and sometimes on the lives of others.

How will you know what the right choice is in any given situation? The ultimate guarantee of making the right choice is to seek God's advice. His advice will sometimes come through His Word, the Bible, other people, or a thought you may have confirming what you believe His answer to you is. But here are a few things that guarantee a wrong choice:

1. The wrong choice breaks rules, regulations, and laws
2. The wrong choice can require you to break the law
3. The wrong choice conjures feelings of unhealthy anxiety before making the choice instead of delivering peace
4. The wrong choice can cause you to feel shame

Sometimes you will make the wrong choice, sometimes intentionally and sometimes unintentionally. You know, I can't imagine intentionally making the wrong choice at this point in my life. I cannot! But when I was your age, I did intentionally make choices that landed me in trouble with my parents, choices that cost me valuable time, choices that damaged my relationships with siblings, and choices that changed the course of my life for a bit. But thankfully the consequences of my actions were not dire. Whew! I dodged some bullets. Intentionally making a wrong choice is disregarding your potential and discounts the majesty that is God. When you plan to make a wrong choice, you are taking a risk on beautiful you becoming fractured you. And while fractures can be healed, it takes time and effort that could have been funneled to preparing for dynamic future you. And while wrong unintentional choices can cause setbacks, wrong intentional choices almost always cause setbacks.

But you should rejoice in knowing that when you chose to accept Jesus as the Son of the one true God and Lord of your life, it was the greatest thing you have ever done, and it seals your victory in the negative consequences you may face as a result of any bad choice you make.

You even have the choice to choose God or not, and although He wants you to choose Him, He will never force you to choose Him! Never!

> "Behold, I stand at the door and knock. If anyone hears My voice and opens the door, I will come into him, and dine with him and he with Me."
>
> Revelation 3:20

He is knocking on the door of your life and your heart and is waiting for you to respond. He is waiting for you to choose Him. To dine with you is to abide in your presence. To "dine with you" means to connect with you, share with you, have intimate fellowship with you. Think about all the meals you've shared with family and friends. What's happening? You are talking, sharing food, sharing your thoughts and heart. God dearly wants to dine with you. He wants you to choose Him. He wants to enter into a relationship with you that is deeper than your heart can feel, more encompassing than what is most complete to you, and more beautiful than the most brilliant diamond. He wants you, and He wants you to choose Him. When you choose Him, you can rest assured that He guides your decision-making and your choices. This is not to say you will not make mistakes; you will many times over make mistakes. Everyone does. But when you are in relationship with God, you will make a practice of basing your decisions and choices on what God's Word, the Bible, says. It will become second nature to you. Others will come to recognize you as an individual of great character simply by the choices you make.

Eleanor Roosevelt once said, "One's philosophy is not best expressed in words; it is best expressed in the choices one makes." What Eleanor Roosevelt meant was who you are as a person, your mantra for life, culminates in the choices you've made. In other words, your life is a result of the choices you've made.

So here is an opportunity for you to think about your past choices and learn from them moving forward. Look at the choices you are faced with making today and really take a few moments to decide the best course of action based on what the Bible says. Your choices should be rooted in honesty, kindness, courage, bravery, resolve, integrity, and a myriad of other things that mirror Jesus' character.

Most importantly, know that sometimes the choice you feel most strongly about or the one you think will make you happiest is not always the best one for you, which is why making a habit of communing with the Father on a regular basis is beneficial to you. The more you abide in His Word and in His presence, the more you will begin to know what choices to make concerning your life.

If you are unsure about a choice or decision you have to make, consult a trusted friend whose values and thinking align with yours. The friend who has in the past expressed a reliance on God. Sometimes God will deliver answers to you through something a trusted friend will say.

Many times, my mother has served as a source of great support in a big decision I've had to make or a choice I've had to make. Your parents have lived much longer than you have and undoubtedly have experienced a lot of the same things you are currently experiencing. Recognize them as a wealth of knowledge, wisdom, and understanding. They are riddled with massive amounts of information and resources you should surely use to enrich your life.

When my daughters were very young, my husband and I decided to have them homeschooled. We felt that I could do a good job of teaching them everything they needed academically to become equipped college students. After all, since before the day each of them was born, I had set the foundation for early learning, reading to them every single day. Once they were old enough to talk, I began teaching them Spanish, science, math, and geography just for fun, filling up their playtime. Sometimes during dinner, my husband reveled in listening to everything they had learned. I was thrilled about our decision and enthusiastically converted the game room in our home to a school, complete with desks, a chalkboard, a computer station, and a small library, everything we needed to succeed. Are you getting the picture? I was a rockstar of a wannabe teacher. We had a very structured day, rising early to have breakfast together. I also built into our day allowing for lunchtime and recess as well because good teachers do. Sometimes for recess we would invite other families to join us on the small manmade lake behind our house to fish! It was wonderful, this homeschooling thing! I was having such fun. Until...one day after about a year, I was clearing things away after what I thought was a very successful homeschooling day, and Kierstin came into the room looking very forlorn with her countenance bearing the brunt of it, head down and shoulders slumped.

She said, "Mommy, I want to go to school with other kids." I gasped. I turned to look at her; her head still hung low as if she were searching the carpet for something lost. I said, "Oh, honey, you like homeschooling, and you're so good at it!" She shook her head yes but, still searching the carpet, did an about-face and left the room as soon as she had entered it.

I thought, *Hmmm, that was strange.* I immediately began to feel I wasn't doing a good job of homeschooling, so I planned to increase my efforts. But days later turned into weeks later of an unsettling feeling in my gut. Did I have a choice to make? I prayed. *Do I disregard Kierstin's desire to be with other kids on a daily basis to continue homeschooling, or do I listen to her sweet, small voice in my ear each day tugging at my heart?* My husband and I prayed as I continued to homeschool the girls for another three to five months, thinking Kierstin had forgotten or didn't really mean she wanted to go to a traditional school with other kids. How could she? Everything was perfect. I was happy. She was happy. Everyone was happy!

Then, in the middle of the most beautiful day ever, Kierstin said, "Mommy, when will I be starting the real school with the other kids?" There it was. The choice we had to make. The choice to continue to fulfill my desire to homeschool her or the choice to allow her to attend a traditional school. My husband and I needed to be careful with that choice. We had to weigh the pros and cons of her attending a school and weigh the message we would be sending to Kierstin if we denied her request without considering her position. The moment was much bigger than her wanting to attend school. Through countless hours of teaching, I had taught her empowerment in making her own choices. She was teaching me how to trust those choices.

We began the process of enrolling her in "real school" the next day. It was one of the best choices we made after much prayer. I watched Kierstin transition from a shy, introverted girl to one who is funny, engaging, and outgoing. Both girls have always exceeded their grade level academics, and they keep our home packed with many of their friends. Kierstin wanted to continue learning but desired socialization. Sometimes our choices are a scream for what we need and for what our hearts desire.

Daughter, remember to pause a moment in your day to pray a moment from your heart as you ask God, the Father, to ordain your choices. You will see your life illumine with Him because your choices are founded in what He thinks about the matters of your life!

## Wearing Emeralds

What choices are you met with having to make today? Write those in the spaces below. Then go to the Word of God to find out what God will say about choice.

_____

_____

_____

_____

_____

_____

_____

_____

_____

_____

_____

_____

_____

_____

_____

_____

_____

_____

_____

_____

_____

_____

## Word Power

Wise: *Having or showing experience, knowledge, and good judgment.*

Are you willing to write about a time in your life you made a choice that wasn't wise and it caused you or someone you know harm?

_____

_____

_____

_____

_____

_____

_____

_____

_____

_____

_____

_____

_____

_____

_____

_____

_____

_____

_____

_____

Cassie Stober
For Reagan

*"Friends come into our lives like nature. Some are annuals, and we enjoy them for only a season. Some are evergreens, and they are consistently dependable and always there for us. We may grieve the loss of someone but can also celebrate what God gives us each season."*

# CHAPTER 29

# Your Losses

*Restored*

Dear Daughter, losses are hard to bear. They are. Maybe you have experienced the loss of a loved one, a friendship, or a loss in a circumstance of life. Experiencing loss is natural in life, and everyone has had a time in their lives when loss has injected itself into their lives. Unfortunately, everyone will lose something from the moment they enter this world to the time they leave it. Some losses can be regained, while others cannot. For example, if you experience the loss of a loved one, someone who has died and gone to heaven, you lose that person's presence on earth forever. An example of a loss that can be regained is when someone loses an opportunity, hair, money, etc. Nevertheless, losses can leave you feeling sad, angry, lost, afraid, hopeless, and uncertain about your future. That's the simple truth of the matter. But another part of that truth is God is still in control, and He did not abandon you in your loss; rather, He is standing with you. You may be asking yourself, "If God was there in my loss, then why didn't He do something to prevent it?" When it comes to loss, that's a question many people ask; those who believe in God, those unsure of God, and those who don't believe in God have all lost something so great they have asked this very question. Have you?

Evil did not originate from God, nor did God create evil. God created the world perfectly and created Adam and Eve perfectly. As we discussed in an earlier chapter, He loved us so much that He created us with free will, the ability to make choices for ourselves. As a result, way back in the garden of Eden, Adam and Eve chose to disobey God's instructions and succumbed to Satan, in the form of a serpent, urging Eve to eat fruit from a tree God had told them to avoid.

The Bible tells us in Genesis:

> Now the serpent was more crafty than any beast of the field which the LORD God had made. And he said to the woman, "Indeed, has God said, 'You shall not eat from any tree of the garden'?" The woman said to the serpent, "From the fruit of the trees of the garden we may eat; but from the fruit of the tree, which is in the middle of the garden, God has said, 'You shall not eat from it or touch it, or you will die.'" The serpent said to the woman, "You surely will not die! For God knows that in the day you eat from it your eyes will be opened, and you will be like God, knowing good and evil."
>
> Genesis 3:1–5

God created Adam and Eve with free will, not like robots who are told what to do. The day Adam and Eve ate from the forbidden tree was the beginning of our choices affecting our lives. Our choices indeed have consequences, and some of those consequences carry a heavy price to pay! Loss.

When Adam and Eve ate of the forbidden fruit, God told them that very thing: that their disobedience would cause them consequences so great that their lives would change forever. He told Adam that from that point on, he would work till the land to earn a living. Eve would have pain in childbirth. So, you see, evil entered into the world by Adam and Eve's disobedience to God. We live in a fallen, sinful world, and people's choices cause consequences that sometimes create loss. One of the biggest consequences of Adam and Eve's sin was death. Their sin determined that we would no longer live forever on earth but would die. Only those living righteously would live again in heaven.

Girl, God is in the midst of your loss despite how you may be feeling. He is standing with you. You are not alone.

"The righteous cry out and the Lord hears and delivers them out of all their troubles. The Lord is near to the brokenhearted and saves those who are crushed in spirit" (Psalm 34:17–18).

I remember the day my mother died was sudden and was without regard. It felt devastatingly unfair and crude. I wasn't ready to say good-bye. I never got the chance. Death didn't care that I loved her so much. It didn't care that my heart would ache for the years that would follow. It didn't care.

The foremost thing to remember about loss is that you can overcome it because God is taking the broken parts of you and restoring them to the parts of you that are still ever present. He will bring the miraculous into your space to speak to you that He is with you. That's what happened to me. He brought the miraculous.

About a year after my mother's passing, I lost my Bible. The Bible I use each Sunday in church to follow along with the sermon. The Bible I use to read during Bible study. The very Bible my mother had given to me when I left for college more than thirty years prior. I no longer had her signature at the end of a short note she had written to me inside the front cover. I was devastated.

When we lose things that we've held dear to us for a long period of time and one that connects one part of our lives to another it seems a double felt loss. I wondered what the message to me was. What did this mean?

I was certain I had lost the Bible in church while attending a women's conference when I couldn't find it anywhere at home. I searched everywhere and had everyone helping. I called the church's lost and found to ask if it had been turned in. The young lady assisting me sent the security guard to the section of the church where I had been sitting. A short while after, she called to say that search was unsuccessful. That night I cried myself to sleep as I prayed to find my Bible. Loss had consumed my spirit, and a period of mourning my mother began all over again. From time to time throughout the years, the thought of my Bible would share the space with thoughts of my mother. And then, five years and some months later, I received a phone call from a young lady from my church. I assumed it was to confirm my presence at a small group session. She asked if I was

Julie, and I responded yes. I thought, *Wait! She just called me Julie*. She then stated that she had my Bible. I gasped. More than five years later? What? Impossible! I very hesitantly asked if she was sure it was mine because the inscription on the front of my Bible said J. Khris Ferland. I asked how she came to think the Bible she had was mine. She responded that she had accessed the membership rolls looking for a Khris Ferland because that was on the front of the Bible, but only Julie Ferland was listed as a member of the church. She then opened to the front inside cover and read the inscription my mother had written to me. My mother always began notes to me referring to me as Julie, my first name, when the whole world knows me as Khris, my middle name. Wow, right?

Loss is bitter, but God will restore you and your loss. "Now to him who is able to do far more abundantly beyond all that we ask or think, according to the power that works within us" (Ephesians 3:20). When you lose friendship, He will bring thirty more potential friends that will be much better suited for you than the one lost. When you lose an opportunity, He is perfectly fashioning the one He ordained for you. When you lose love, He will bring Himself to you in a greater measure and display the love you lost, which will leave you feeling renewed in love.

You can be restored and made to feel whole again. Yes! I miss my mother dearly, but I know that one day I will see her again in heaven because she knows God and accepts Jesus as God's Son. That is what comforts me and makes me smile. Loss can be overcome.

Loss is very real, and it is felt quite deeply. Loss can affect a person for a long time because something or someone that has been a part of our lives for such a long time is suddenly gone, sometimes without warning. One begins to mourn that loss immediately. God Himself feels the pain of your loss. The Bible tells us He feels what we feel. He is a compassionate, caring God who heals. You may be feeling as though your loss is something you cannot overcome. Your heart may be breaking and your countenance sad. You will miss seeing your loved one who no longer lives on this earth, the severed friendship has you feeling lonely, and the loss of hope in a dream is swelling so largely you can no longer feel what hoping is like. But our Father hears your cries, even the ones that come in the deepest hours of the night when everyone else is asleep. With His own hands, He is creating things for you that will bring you joy. No matter how many tears you cry, they can never overflow the hands of God! Never!

## Wearing Emeralds

Use the space below to write a letter to the loved one you lost or to a friend whose friendship is lost. If you are experiencing loss in a circumstance, write the letter to the circumstance. Express how this loss makes you feel and commit to doing something that will help you feel empowered as you are experiencing loss.

_____

_____

_____

_____

_____

_____

_____

_____

_____

_____

_____

_____

_____

_____

_____

_____

_____

_____

## Word Power

Restored: *Return someone or something to a former condition, place, or position.*

Write about a time you felt a grave loss, but then God brought restoration.

_____

_____

_____

_____

_____

_____

_____

_____

_____

_____

_____

_____

_____

_____

_____

_____

_____

_____

_____

_____

_____

Betina Driver

For Cristina and Charity

*"Your God is always there. He's in the dim light that seeps into the crack of your window at night when you're awakened by a frightening thought. He's in the wind that blows across your cheek on an extremely dry, sweltering day. Be aware, say hello, invite Him to sit or to walk with you. Let your God be your number one companion."*

# CHAPTER 30

# Your God

*Captivating*

Dear Daughter, what do you know about God? Do you ever think about Him? If so, what sorts of thoughts do you have? The average person's perception of God is that He is sitting somewhere high up in the sky, looking down on the earth, ready to exact punishment upon those who are considered "bad." That He judges everything we do ready to send us to "hell" if we do anything remotely egregious. I must say not one of those statements is true, and they ignite such adverse and unfavorable feelings, preventing a possible desire to even get to know Him. I don't want to acquaint myself with someone I've heard has a reputation for judging and punishing others for what He perceives as bad behavior. That is not God!

Think back to the very first time you heard anything about God. What was your very first thought about the character of God? Our first impressions sometimes inevitably take precedence and become that which shape our lives and the standard by which we measure our thinking. Our first thoughts about anything are what we believe until we learn differently through our pursuit of a possibly different perspective or through a natural flow of things unfolding that demonstrates otherwise. Frequently, most people will receive their concept of who God is from other people and not seek the answers from the Bible, God's own words. This is why what they think they know of God hardly ever mirrors the biblical truths, and so they never really know the true character of God nor engage in a relationship with Him.

When you decide wholeheartedly to learn about who God is, you will be captivated by His character and smitten with what He thinks about you. "The Spirit Himself testifies with our spirit that we are children of God, and if children, heirs also, heirs with God and fellow heirs with Christ, if indeed we suffer with Him so that we may also be glorified with Him" (Romans 8:16–17). He calls you daughter and an heir to everything He has and is. You are co-heir with His only Son, Jesus. Once you learn the true character and nature of who God is, you will dance in joy at the fact He calls you His child. You will have a peace so great in knowing that heaven is real. "For our citizenship is in heaven, from which also we eagerly wait for a Savior, the Lord Jesus Christ" (Philippians 3:20).

Building a relationship with God is one of the easiest things you will ever do! If you've ever heard the way to do so is to follow a bunch of rules and regulations, wipe that completely clean from your mind. Getting to know God is not complicated or exhaustive. It is simple, interesting, and fun. But it will require your time. These are some things to think about while learning who God really is:

1. Believe and accept that God's Son is Jesus and that God loved us so much that He sent Jesus to die for us. That "Jesus to die for us" statement is very complex and leaves us thinking, *How? Why?* In short, so that humans could have our sins forgiven and receive eternal life. Not eventually die and that be the end of who we are. "For God so loved the world that he gave his only begotten Son that whosoever believes in him shall not perish but have everlasting life" (John 3:16).

   As my relationship with God grew, I wanted everyone to know! I was proud to know God and wanted God to be happy with me acknowledging His Son. Several years ago, when our family was anticipating moving into our newly built home, my husband asked each of us, the girls and me, what we each wanted to put into the house as a symbolic piece to commemorate our relationship with God and our family's new beginning. After the girls each chose their items, I said I wanted two lions to be placed on the top part of the driveway. One on each side. They all looked at me with questioning faces, but once I got those lions, they understood. It was a witnessing tool when new neighbors came by to welcome our family into the neighborhood. They'd comment on how beautiful the lions were, and I had the opportunity to say, "They symbolize Jesus, the Lion of Judah." The conversations that came out of those times as I tried to explain! I also remember the pizza delivery boy exclaiming, "What's up with the lions?" and the girls, who had accompanied me to the front door to receive the pizza, rolling their eyes back and saying, "Oh no! Why'd you have to ask her that!" I never laughed so hard.

2. Talk to God regularly. Just have conversations about anything you like. Anything. Talk to Him as though you are talking to a friend; that's also who He is to you. Your time to talk to God is your time to be open, honest, and without reserve. Pour your heart out sometimes, and sometimes give thanks. You'll know what moment requires you to do each.

3. Read the Bible. The Bible can be difficult to read and understand, but don't allow that to deter you. Perhaps begin with a Bible study and use the Bible as an accompaniment. Better yet, attend a church Bible study where a teacher is guiding your study.

Daughter, there is only one God. His Son is Jesus Christ. He is an amazing God. He is an indescribable love that reached into the depths of the earth, defying reason, logic, and scope to bring you a clear but sure path unto Himself. He loves you! That path was Jesus' death on the cross, the same path that seals your victory in all circumstances. Your God will blow you away as you get to know Him better as you declare He is Lord of your life.

The gamut of emotions you will feel as you take this journey of discovery will be like a whirlwind lifting you into the waiting arms that are His. He will make you smile; He will make you cry; He will make you angry. He will confuse you and infuse you with Himself when you need Him most! He will hold you up high, protecting you from falls. He will drop you low into your destiny when you seek Him first.

Your God created everything, knows everything, is everywhere, and is all-powerful. There is none like Him, nor will there ever be. As you grow in your relationship with God, you will begin to experience Him in ways you can't imagine. He will become most real to you once you do. When I was your age, I didn't recognize God in my life, but He has always been with me. I look back on moments of discord and mayhem, moments of triumph and victory, moments of peace and solace. He has always been there.

When I was about eight years old, I asked my mother how she knew God was real. You see, I grew up the daughter of a preacher, a pastor of a church, so not going to church was not an option for my six siblings and me. We went to Sunday school, Bible study, and church each week. If there was a special program, we went to that too. We didn't have a choice. I rather enjoyed getting to know this God my parents introduced us to. The idea of Him was comforting to me, and I often stole away to be alone with Him. So, when I asked my mother this question, she was quite taken aback looking down into my wide innocent eyes. Her response was, "Your faith will allow you to experience Him, and then you will surely know." Hmmmmmmmmm. That gave me pause. I didn't get more to that explanation for a long time after that. Until one day I did experience Him. On faith I prayed to Him sometimes just to say hello, other times to thank Him. But on the day I experienced Him, the day I knew for myself God was real, was the day my brother and I were in a car accident on our way home from school. It was raining rather torrentially, and it was impossible for the windshield wipers to divert the rain from the windshield quickly enough. We could barely see the road in front of us, although my brother was driving very slowly and carefully. We never saw the other vehicle coming toward ours but felt the impact as if it were an eighteen-wheeler demolishing our small car. My brother was thrown from the car, and I needed to be cut from it. I was hoping my God could understand the prayer I prayed between the sobs swelling my throat. As I was being cut from the car, the emergency workers kept reassuring me that I was going to be okay. The rain continued its fury, and I continued to question those trying to free me from the car.

"Where is Kip! He's my brother and was driving us home from school," I persisted.

Both emergency workers continued as if they didn't hear my questions between sobs.

"We're going to get you out. You're going to be fine—don't worry!"

Why weren't they answering my questions about my brother? I began to cry even more, not knowing where my brother was. I wanted my brother to live too. I wanted him to be waiting for me outside the car as the emergency medical team tried to free me. I wanted him to know I didn't think any of this was his fault and that I would tell my parents so. So that's what I prayed to my God. And I said, "God, I need to experience You now! Where is my brother? God, I'm told You are the God of the universe, that You made heaven and earth. You can calm this rain, and You can allow Kip to be alive! God, where is my brother!"

Once they freed me from the car and hurled me onto a gurney, the rain started to fall even harder. My eyes fell on what looked like a sack on the side of the road, and my mother was kneeling beside it, touching it. Just as my heart began to sink, it moved, and my brother's head peered from beneath it, his hands reaching up to hold my mother's. My mother was using the tarp to shield my brother from the rain! He was alive, and my God heard my prayer and answered me. My faith allowed me to experience Him. He says in Isaiah 65:24, "It will come to pass that BEFORE they call I will answer and while they are still speaking, I will hear."

Maybe you are asking your own parents or another adult in your life how they know God is real. Undoubtedly, those who know He is real have a story to tell of how He transformed their lives and increased their faith. Perhaps you are seeking to experience Him for yourself. You will if you continue to seek Him.

> "But if from there you will seek the Lord your God, and you will find
> "Him if you search for him with all your heart and with all your soul."
>
> Deuteronomy 4:29 (NASB)

To enter into a relationship with this God of ours, God of the universe, is to cherish yourself and your life. God is not a thing of the imagination we hear great Bible stories about. He is real on a daily basis weaving His mastery into your life. His breath moves the leaves of the trees He created. His hands created fire and balled it up, making the sun. He hung that sun in the vast, sometimes black, sometimes blue, sometimes white, but all the time mighty sky. Mighty because it creates clouds that, when we look up from below, send our imaginations on journeys across that sky. It holds billions upon trillions of stars that illumine the night. And...He...knows...each... one...by...name!

His love overshadows you, and because it does, there is nothing you can do that will make God stop loving you. Nothing! Oh, think about the beauty in that! There is never a need to worry that if you fail, He will no longer love you. He will never leave you. God loves you and is waiting for you to come to Him so that He can bless your life according to his will for your life. Think about it. He only had one Son, Jesus, whom He adored and loved without reserve. But He loved you, too, and sacrificed Jesus so that we could have a chance to live in eternity with Him.

> "He that spared not his own Son, but delivered him up for us all, how shall he not with him also freely give us all things?"
>
> Romans 8:32

Think of your all-time favorite thing in the entire world. Go ahead. Take a moment to do that. Now, think about giving it away so that a friend or someone you don't even know can have it to live a better life. That's essentially what God did for you and me.

There are so many facets to our wonderful God. His character is unquestionable. He is always right no matter who disagrees with Him. He is always working on all things for your good no matter how bad things look. He always wins and gives you victory in the battles you face. God is infinite, always existed and always will. He knows no boundaries. God is holy, pure, sinless, righteous. God is faithful; everything He says He will do, He will do.

Daughter, when you come into the knowledge that God is not a Creator of sin, discord, or tragedy, but man's free will initiates the mayhem we face in life, you will also appreciate God and His sovereignty. You will. How else are we saved from the chaos and tumult of this world?

Psalm 46:1–3 reminds us, "God is our refuge and strength, A very present help in trouble. Therefore, we will not fear, though the earth should change, and though the mountains slip into the heart of the sea, Though its waters roar and foam, Though the mountains quake at its swelling pride."

There are so many names for God, and each one describes a part of His nature:

He is El Shaddai—God Almighty
He is El Elyon—the Most High God
He is El Olam—the Everlasting God
He is Yahweh—God Independent and Self Sufficient
He is Theos—the Only True God, Unique and Transcendent
He is Adonai—God as Master, Authority, Provider

He is so amazing, and I wish for you to know Him even more. When you are on your journey to get to know Him, you will smile more, laugh more, sing more, and dance more. Your life won't be without challenges, but He will be in the midst. You see, He is always with you and provides the strength you need, the courage, the bravery, the guidance, the hope, the grace, the love, the joy you need to look in the eyes of any problem, any trial, any test and say, "I am delighted to know Jesus' Father, the one true God. He is my Father too!"

So go for it! Begin your journey to know El Elyon, the Most High God. He is worth it and welcomes it. He is excited for you and excited about you. He, indeed, is your Father too!

## Wearing Emeralds

Where do you grow from here? Write below how you will continue your journey to discover who you are in Christ.

Think of a few people who you would like to ask the question, "How do you know God is real?" Write their responses next to their names in the spaces below.

_____

_____

_____

_____

_____

_____

_____

_____

_____

_____

_____

_____

_____

_____

_____

_____

## Word Power

Captivating: *Capable of attracting and holding interest, charming.*

Why do you think God would be captivated by you?

_____

_____

_____

_____

_____

_____

_____

_____

_____

_____

_____

_____

_____

_____

_____

_____

_____

_____

_____

# Afterword

Mothers can be strange creatures. We can be fiercely protective of our children one minute, supremely proud of their achievements the next, and madly annoyed with them after that. And in those three minutes we have the ability to career from maternal conviction to desperate self-doubt.

We were also built to give birth. For all the imagery—and experience—of nurturance and intimacy linked to motherhood, birthing is usually nothing short of an epic encounter that would frighten a gladiator. Let us not be euphemistic. It is a struggle. So *Your Destiny Begins with Identity: 30 Things God Wants Every Girl to Know Now*, written by a mother of two, is naturally a work of tenderness and struggle/intensity, giggles and exhortation, hopes and fears.

But why fears? Because ladies-in-waiting, from every screen and in every soundbite, messages are bombarding you with suggestions about who you are and who you should become. And society has a suggestion for every day of the year. It can be confusing. Above all the cacophony and buzz, one thing only is true: you should be everything God made you to be. Everything. Nothing more, nothing less.

"Everything God made you to be" is what this book is about. Here, in thirty chapters, you have had the distinct pleasure of peeping into the diversity, depth, and drama of what it means to become a daughter of distinction. Written by one of "us." A mother. Hopefully your expectations lock away dreams to be let loose, your imagination to do a cartwheel of joy, and your faith in the God who designed you to ignite a new fire of purpose. Take these tools you've learned and continue the journey, my daughter. Continue the journey and enjoy.

Anthea Henderson, PhD
Communicator, media consultant, and podcaster

"The father of boys, I had the privilege to coach girls for many years. I felt a calling that each one was God's gift to direct, protect, and support. I found it interesting that through teaching them to compete, I learned they became empowered. I hope their power frames their lives well after sports and is the foundation of their love for Christ as they seek to learn their identity in Him."

Darrell Johnson

Mothers, if this book is a gift to your daughter, write a letter to her here.

Daughters, write a letter to your mother.

_____

_____

_____

_____

_____

_____

_____

_____

_____

_____

_____

_____

_____

_____

_____

_____

_____

_____

_____

# Endnotes

1   Douglas D. Burmana, Tali Bitanc, and James R. Booth, "Study: A Biological Reason Why Girls Have Better Language Skills than Boys," published March 3, 2008, https://www.science20.com/news_releases/study_a_biological_reason_why_girls_have_better_language_skills_than_boys; Peter Aldhous, "Why Women Are Better with Words," *New Scientist*, February 18, 1995, https://www.newscientist.com/article/mg14519651-500-why-women-are-better-with-words/; IntelligentHQ, "Are Women Better at Learning Languages than Men?" https://www.intelligenthq.com/are-women-better-at-learning-languages-than-men/

2   Malcolm Gladwell, *Outliers: The Story of Success* (New York: Little, Brown and Company, 2008)

3   Madhuleena Roy Chowdhury, "The Neuroscience of Gratitude and Effects on the Brain, published April 9, 2019, https://positivepsychology.com/neuroscience-of-gratitude/

# About the Author

Khris Ferland is a former television news anchor and reporter for an NBC affiliate in the panhandle of Texas. Answering God's call, she left the news industry to raise her daughters and began her journey to empower girls. Khris is driven by her profound love for words and the art of crafting them to inspire and uplift. Her dedication to designing words that positively impact the lives of women and girls is the cornerstone of her work now. Through her writing and speaking, she aims to instill confidence, resilience, and self-worth in women and girls, helping them navigate the challenges of life with grace and purpose. Khris works in the women's ministry of her home church and serves as an integral part. She lives in a suburb of Dallas, Texas, with her husband and two daughters.

Printed in the USA
CPSIA information can be obtained
at www.ICGtesting.com
CBHW070936110724
11410CB00021B/870